Exceptional Cars

Maserati 4CLT

Porter Press International

Also published by Porter Press International

The Jaguar Portfolio
Ultimate E-type – The Competition Cars
Jaguar E-type – The Definitive History (2nd edition)
Original Jaguar XK (3rd edition)
Jaguar Design – A Story of Style
Saving Jaguar

Original Scrapbooks
Stirling Moss Scrapbook 1929-1954
Stirling Moss Scrapbook 1955
Stirling Moss Scrapbook 1956-1960
Stirling Moss Scrapbook 1961
Graham Hill Scrapbook 1929-1966
Murray Walker Scrapbook
Martin Brundle Scrapbook
Barry Cryer Comedy Scrapbook

Great Cars series
No. 1 – Jaguar Lightweight E-type – the autobiography of 4 WPD
No. 2 – Porsche 917 – the autobiography of 917-023
No. 3 – Jaguar D-type – the autobiography of XKD 504
No. 4 – Ferrari 250GT SWB – the autobiography of 2119 GT
No. 5 – Maserati 250F – the autobiography of 2528
No. 6 – ERA – the autobiography of R4D
No. 7 – Ferrari 250GTO – the autobiography of 4153 GT
No. 8 – Jaguar Lightweight E-type – the autobiography of 49 FXN
No. 9 – Jaguar C-type – the autobiography of XKC 051
No. 10 – Lotus 18 – the autobiography of Stirling Moss's '912'
No. 11 – Ford GT40 – the autobiography of 1075
No. 12 – Alfa Romeo Monza – the autobiography of the celebrated 2211130

Exceptional Cars series
No. 1 - Iso Bizzarrini - the remarkable history of A3/C 0222
No. 2 - Jaguar XK120 - the remarkable history of JWK 651
No. 3 - Ford GT40 MkII- the remarkable history of 1016
No. 4 - The First Three Shelby Cobras
No.5 - Aston Martin Ulster - the remarkable history of CMC 614

Porter Profiles
No. 1 - Austin Healey - the story of DD 300

Deluxe leather-bound, signed, limited editions with slipcases are available for most titles.
Books available from retailers or signed copies direct from the publisher.
To order simply phone +44 (0)1584 781588, fax +44 (0)1584 781630, visit the website or email sales@porterpress.co.uk

Keep up-to-date with news about current books and new releases at:
www.porterpress.co.uk

Exceptional Cars

Maserati 4CLT
The remarkable history of chassis no. 1600

Cristián Bertschi

Consultant: Adam Ferrington

Porter Press International

©Cristián Bertschi

All rights reserved. No part of this publication may be reproduced, stored in a retrieval system or transmitted, in any form or by any means, electronic, mechanical, photocopying, recording or otherwise, without prior permission in writing from the publisher

First published in February 2019

978-1-907085-75-8

Published by
Porter Press International Ltd

Hilltop Farm, Knighton-on-Teme, Tenbury Wells, WR15 8LY, UK
Tel: +44 (0)1584 781588   Fax: +44 (0)1584 781630
sales@porterpress.co.uk
www.porterpress.co.uk

Edited by Ray Hutton
Design & Layout by Andrew Garman

Printed by Gomer Press Ltd

COPYRIGHT

We have made every effort to trace and acknowledge copyright holders and we apologise in advance for any unintentional omission. We would be pleased to insert the appropriate acknowledgement in any subsequent edition.

Contents

Foreword		7
Introduction		9

The Car — 10

| 1 | From Voiturette to Formula 1 | 12 |
| 2 | The racing career of the 4CL and 4CLT | 20 |

The Races of 4CLT 1600 — 34

| 3 | 1949: ACA's first international season | 36 |
| 4 | 1950: Fangio scores 1600's greatest victory | 52 |

Transplant: 1600 with a Ford V8 — 68

| 5 | Rebirth for Mecánica Nacional Fuerza Libre | 70 |
| 6 | Racing career with Juan Viaggio | 74 |

Found and restored — 80

7	Mystery in Argentina	82
8	Back to the track	88
9	Owning and driving 1600	100
10	Photo gallery	108

Acknowledgements	126
Index	127

Foreword

by Rubén Juan Fangio

The invitation from Ton Blankvoort to visit Silverstone in July was unexpected but truly delightful. It was the first time that Oscar 'Cacho' Fangio and I had had the opportunity to see the car in which our father achieved early success when he first travelled to Europe, 70 years ago.

What a joy to see the Maserati in the blue and yellow racing colours of Argentina, with JM Fangio emblazoned on its flanks! And what a privilege to be asked to add our signatures under his name!

Juan Manuel Fangio, five-times World Champion, was a hero throughout Argentina. He brought recognition and prestige to a country that, at that time, was not well known in many parts of the world.

There is a further connection that makes this Maserati more special to us. The Fangio family originated in Italy in the Abruzzi region; our paternal grandfather emigrated to Argentina at the age of seven. And when the Automóvil Club Argentino sent a team to Europe, it was based in Italy, where our father always felt at home.

It is marvellous that this book has been produced to celebrate one of the most significant cars in Juan Manuel Fangio's racing career and we are very proud to be in some small way associated with it.

● A proud moment. Maserati 4CLT 1600 is autographed by Fangio's two sons at Silverstone, July 2018. Oscar adds his signature as Rubén occupies the seat of the car that brought their father two early Grand Prix victories. *Ton Blankvoort collection*

Introduction

A message at the entrance to the Simeone Foundation in Philadelphia states: 'Motor racing started when the second car was built'. That was the case in Argentina. In the early years of the automobile, wealthy individuals imported cars from Europe and America. Once the second one arrived, there were two racers being driven at full throttle. Thus started Argentina's continuing strong passion for motor racing.

Through European immigration of the last decades of the 19th century and the first of the 20th, Argentina had established itself as a prime exporter of meat and corn to the rest of the world, especially Europe. Agriculture had a predominant role in the economy and the land was owned by only a few families. That land translated into great wealth.

Immigration brought not only people but a lot of culture: music, fashion and food, also art, architecture and design. It was very common for these wealthy families to bring an architect from Europe to design and build a house in the style of, for example, a French palace. When it came to cars, obtaining the best from overseas was somewhat easier: just put them on a boat, perhaps with the furniture for the new house, and ship to Buenos Aires.

At the end of the Second World War everything changed. On 4 June 1946, General Juan Domingo Perón was elected President. He came to change many things in society, and sport was a way to build a feeling of being part of something: nationalism. With the leit motif *'Perón apoya el deporte'* ('Perón supports sports'), athletic disciplines became popular. Sports personalities rose to prominence: Delfo Cabrera won the Olympic marathon in 1948, heavyweight weight-lifter Humberto Selvetti gained a silver medal in 1952, and golfer Roberto de Vicenzo won his first World Cup in 1953.

But of all sports, motor racing was Perón's favourite. So he decided to organize a race for Grand Prix cars at the beginning of 1947, inviting Italian drivers including Luigi Villoresi, Achille Varzi and Carlo Maria Pintacuda with their own cars. It was the start of a new era in Argentina and was to put the country on the world stage for motor racing.

Soon, Argentina had a number of race circuits, mostly through streets or parks. Its drivers were competing side-by-side with the Europeans but needed up-to-date cars. Perón wanted to support the most talented local drivers. The Automóvil Club Argentino was perfect for this purpose, which is why and how top cars like Maserati 4CLTs and Ferrari 166FLs were raced in blue and yellow during the late 1940s and early 1950s.

Maserati 4CLT serial number 1600, the subject of this book, was one of the leading actors in this rich era of motor racing and a springboard to Europe for the great Argentinian drivers Juan Manuel Fangio and Froilán González.

Cristián Bertschi, Buenos Aires, December 2018

● International motor racing came to Argentina with the staging of the Temporadas ('seasons'), including street races where the enthusiastic crowds were barely constrained. Here, two Maserati 4CLTs fight for the lead at Rosario in 1950.
Ton Blankvoort collection

Maserati 4CLT chassis number 1600 as it is today, resplendent in the blue and yellow Argentine racing colours. It was one of two cars delivered to the Automóvil Club Argentino in 1949 and raced for two seasons in Europe and South America.
Pim van der Maden

Part 1
The car

The Maserati 4CLT was a vitally important Grand Prix car in the immediate post-war period. The dominant Alfa Romeo 158 – the Alfetta - was run only by the factory and Ferrari had yet to reach the heights it would later achieve. Maserati, a company that was regularly in financial difficulties, found its place supplying and encouraging private teams. The 4CLT, like the 4CL that preceded it, was available to anyone who wanted to buy.

One eager customer was the Automóvil Club Argentino, which with the support of President Juan Perón acquired two Maserati 4CLTs to put Argentine drivers on the international stage and enhance the country's prestige. One of those 4CLTs was numbered 1600 and is the subject of this book.

The 4CLT evolved directly from the pre-war 4CL that was created for the 1939 season to compete in the voiturette class. This class was limited to half the engine displacement of the current 3-litre Grand Prix cars.

The 4CL engine was a single-stage supercharged 1.5-litre four-cylinder, developing around 220bhp. That was about 50bhp more than its six-cylinder predecessor, the 6CM, thanks to the adoption of a 16-valve cylinder head, larger Roots-type blower and higher compression.

In 1947 Maserati experimented with a tubular chassis for the 4CL and two-stage supercharging. Both were incorporated in the 4CLT (the T for Tubolare) which made its début at the 1948 San Remo Grand Prix and scored a resounding win. It was known thereafter as the Maserati San Remo.

Chapter 1
From Voiturette to Formula 1

With the big players in pre-war Grand Prix racing like Mercedes-Benz and Alfa Romeo being supported by the German and Italian governments, Maserati had to take a different direction. It decided to concentrate on the voiturette ('small car') category.

For the 1938 season Alfa Romeo presented its new contender built to the voiturette rules for cars with 1,500cc engine capacity. It was called the Alfa Romeo 158, but became better known as the 'Alfetta'. Alfa Romeo was then competing in both the Grand Prix and voiturette classes with an array of different cars with 3-litre engines, the 308, 312 and 316 (in reference to the engine size and number of cylinders) and the eight-cylinder 158.

Maserati continued with its existing breed of racers, producing a replacement for the 1.5-litre six-cylinder 6CM Corsa Monoposto. The 4CL was the new link in the chain of single-seaters that lead to the 4CLT.

The 6CM

The Maserati 6CM was built from 1936 to 1940. Fewer than 30 cars were produced using the 4CM frame and the front suspension from the V8RI model. The engine was an in-line six-cylinder with 65mm bore and 75mm stroke, compression ratio of 6:1, double overhead camshafts, two valves per cylinder, and a Roots-type supercharger.

The chassis was of ladder-type and the body was very recognizable as a Maserati for its overall shape and the bulbous grille. A four-speed gearbox transmitted the engine's power to a live rear axle suspended on semi-elliptic leaf springs with friction dampers. At the front there were torsion bars with friction dampers. Four drums were in charge of stopping the car. Its overall weight was around 650kg.

The 6CM was introduced to the public at the Milan Motor Show in 1936 and the first version developed around 155bhp at 6,200rpm. Later developments brought the power output for 1939 to 175bhp at 6,600rpm. Many 6CMs were sold to privateers, Scuderia Ambrosiana being one of the most successful teams.

The 4CL

A new four-cylinder contender for the 1,500cc class was introduced in 1939 and about 15 units were built by 1946, with the obvious interruption during the war years. The in-line six of the 6CM was no longer competitive and as the new car had to race against the Alfettas and the British ERAs, it had to be as advanced as possible.

The new engine was a 'square' in-line four-cylinder, with 78mm of bore and stroke, and a compression ratio of 6.5:1. Double overhead camshafts and four valves per cylinder were fed by a Roots-type supercharger with a Weber 45 DCO carburettor. The 1,491cc engine produced about 220bhp at 8,000rpm.

The engine was mounted longitudinally at the front of a ladder-type chassis frame. Front suspension was by double wishbones, torsion bars and Houdaille friction dampers and the live rear axle had semi-elliptic leaf springs and Houdaille friction dampers. One of the 4CL's weak points was the worm-and-peg steering which was slow and not very accurate in response. Brakes were the usual drums on all four wheels and the gearbox was a Fiat-derived four-speed. The body

● Maserati factory drawings of the layout of the 4CLT, as introduced in 1948. The live axle and rear suspension were carried over from the 4CL but the front suspension, by double wishbones and coil springs was new.

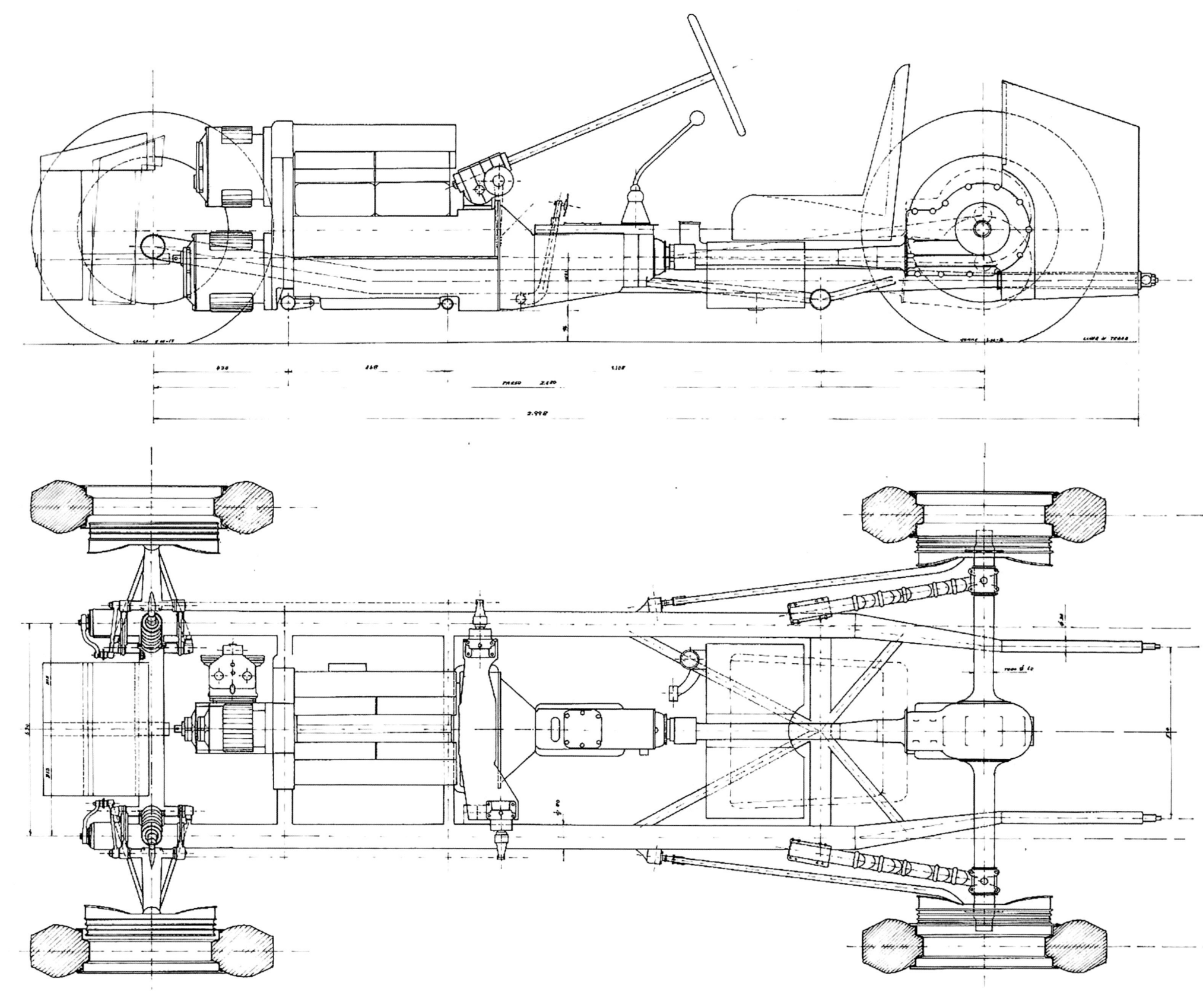

From Voiturette to Formula 1

- Origins – the Maserati 6CM, with a supercharged six-cylinder engine, was introduced in 1936 and was the forerunner of the 4CL and 4CLT. Compare its outward similarity with the 4CL on the page opposite. *The Spitzley Zagari Collection*

was made in aluminium and the total weight was around 630kg.

The 4CL was very successful, especially in minor races in the hands of privateers, and also in bigger events driven by figures such as Luigi Villoresi, but it was not fully competitive with the Alfetta, which had a tubular chassis and a twin-supercharged engine, as well as full support from the factory.

The 4CLT

What was called 4CLT or 4CLT/48 - or simply the San Remo - is a direct evolution of the 4CL. Since 1946, Maserati had been experimenting with a tubular frame fitted with the 4CL engine. For the 1947 Temporada in Argentina, Luigi Villoresi had some success in an interim car run by Scuderia Ambrosiana with a tubular frame but the unchanged single-stage supercharged 4CL engine. The car was fast and reliable but the only opposition he

From Voiturette to Formula 1

The 4CL, with a new dohc 16-valve four-cylinder engine, at the Maserati factory prior to its first race in Tripoli in 1939. *The Spitzley Zagari Collection*

had came from the experienced Achille Varzi with his heavy 1938 Alfa Romeo 12C/316.

The official début of the new Maserati *monoposto* was in San Remo on 27 June 1948 with a fantastic win by Alberto Ascari. Although it was clearly a development of the 4CL, the 4CLT was a big jump ahead. The 1,491cc DOHC engine used the same 78mm x 78mm cylinder dimensions but with a big Weber 50 DCO carburettor in place of the 45 DCO. The single supercharger was replaced by a two-stage system with two Roots-type blowers. The result was about 260bhp at 7,000rpm.

The main change was the chassis frame. It was built with longitudinal tubes and tubular cross-members. This was a stronger and more rigid structure than the 4CL's ladder frame and allowed the suspension to work better. The front suspension was by double wishbones with coil springs, while at the rear there was a live axle with semi-elliptic leaf springs. Houdaille hydraulic dampers were used front and rear.

Maserati 4CLT | 15

From Voiturette to Formula 1

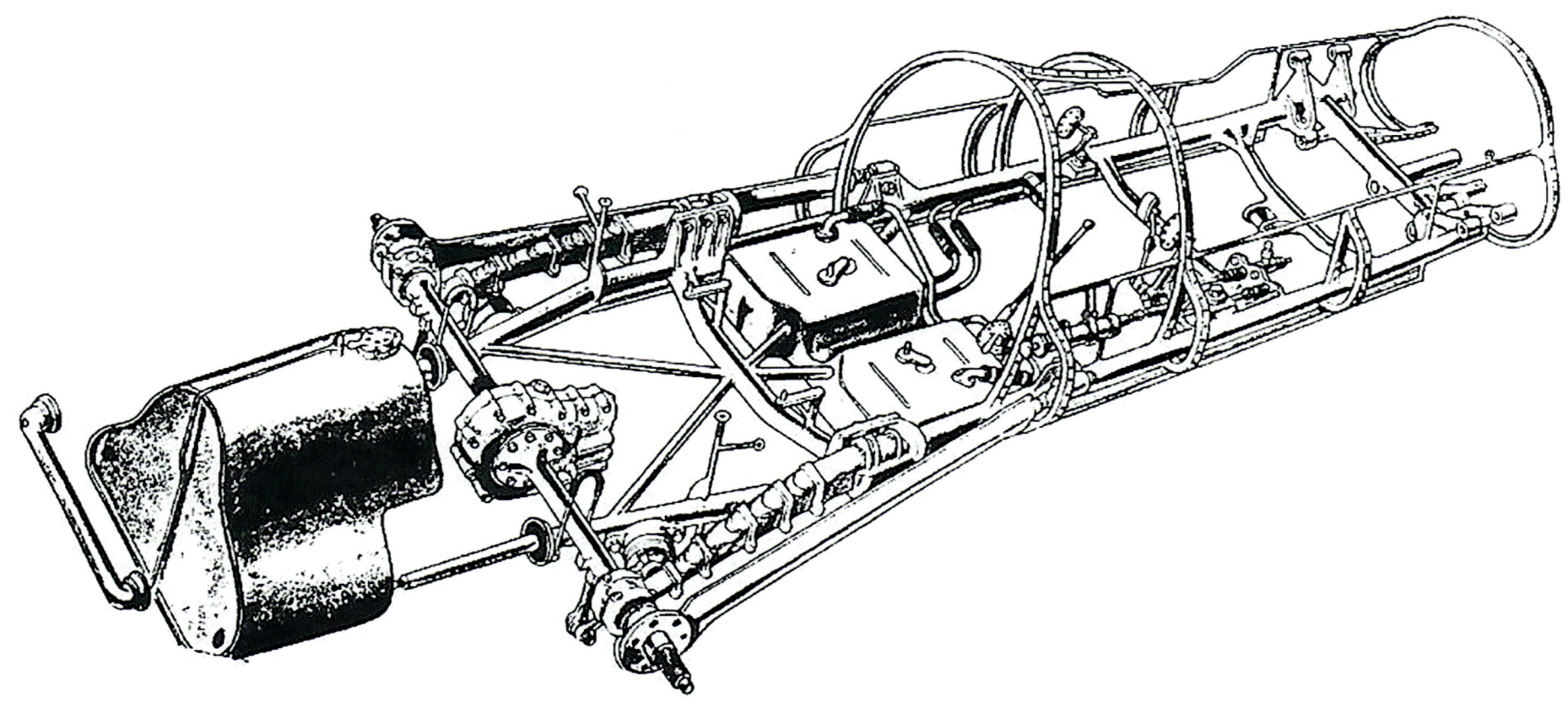

- The tubular chassis that really made the difference for the 4CLT. In this drawing, note the engine oil tank is amidships and the 190-litre fuel tank outrigged in the tail.

While other teams were still using leaf springs for front suspension, the adoption of double wishbones and coil springs proved to be a very good option. Hydraulically-operated drum brakes were standard fit for competitive race cars of the time. The worst parts of the new car were the old gearbox that was very slow and the worm-gear steering that still did not have the desirable accuracy. The new, more slender body shape, with the radiator re-positioned, made the car more streamlined and allowed it to reach a top speed of around 270km/h (168mph).

Good results in the 4CLT's first two years encouraged further development. So for the 1950 season a modified car was introduced, designated 4CLT/50. The improvements included revised brake drums for better cooling, some minor changes to the cockpit, and, the most visible, the oil tank re-positioned on the right side of the car with the cap on the outside of the bodywork.

Most attention for 1950 was expended on the engine. Bigger superchargers and a new crankshaft were amongst the items that were re-worked, bringing the maximun power to around 280bhp, which was similar to the outputs of its main rivals. The car's weight was slightly reduced and in consequence the top speed was a little higher.

These were the last developments for the 4CLT. The next step in the series of Maserati single-seaters would be the A6GCM and then the ultimate Maserati Grand Prix car, the 250F.

From Voiturette to Formula 1

4CLT rear suspension (right) is by angled leaf springs. Brake drums have deep fins for cooling, assisted at the front by inner air ducts (below). *Tony Merrick*

Maserati 4CLT | 17

From Voiturette to Formula 1

SPECIFICATION 4CLT/48 F1

Chassis/body: steel tubular frame with longitudinal and cross-members, aluminium body panels

Engine: 1,491cc, in-line four-cylinder with double overhead camshafts and four-valves-per-cylinder. Two Roots superchargers, Weber 50 DCO carburettor, Compression ratio 6.0:1

Power: 260hp @ 7,000rpm

Transmission: four-speed with reverse, no syncromesh

Clutch: dry, multi-plate

Steering: worm-and-peg

Suspension, front: double wishbones, coil springs, Houdaille hydraulic shock absorbers

Suspension, rear: semi-elliptic leaf springs, trailing arms, Houdaille hydraulic shock absorbers

Brakes: hydraulic, drums

Wheels front/rear: wire-spoked, 3.25-17, 4.00-16

Tyres, front/rear: 5.25-17, 6.00-16

Wheelbase: 2,500mm (98.4in)

Track, front/rear: 1,250mm/1,200mm (49.2in/47.2in)

Length: 3,820mm (150.4in)

Weight: 630kg (1,389lb)

Maximum speed: 260-270km/h (162-168mph)

● The two-stage supercharged engine of 4CLT 1600, as first raced in Argentina in 1949 (top) and after restoration, when the car arrived in England in 1996 (left). *whitefly.cc/Tony Merrick*

1600 without bodywork after an extensive ● rebuild by Rainer Ott in 2012. Note the oil tank relocated on the side of the chassis, one of the modifications made for the 1950 season. *Rainer Ott*

Exceptional Cars

Chapter 2
The racing career of the 4CL and 4CLT

The 4CL made its début at the Grand Premio di Tripoli on 7 May 1939, driven by Luigi Villoresi. Driving a special car with an all-enveloping body, very unusual for a single-seater, the Italian driver took pole position ahead of the Mercedes-Benz W165s of Hermann Lang and Rudolf Caracciola and the Alfa Romeo of Giuseppe Farina.

Tripoli had the largest entry of any voiturette race, with 30 cars on the starting grid, including six Alfettas, four works Maseratis, and three new Mercedes-Benz – which were making their first and last pre-war appearance. Most impressive is the number of Maseratis that took part: 22 cars including 4CLs, 4CMs and 6CMs.

The race was completely dominated by the new Mercedes. Villoresi lost the lead at the start, and the two W165s of Lang and Caracciola ran out-front, on their own. It was a very hot day and all the Italian cars suffered: the Alfas overheated and had to abandon one after the other; the streamlined Maserati of the pole man and the other two 4CLs of Giovanni Rocco and Count Carlo Felice Trossi retired with engine problems. It was a bittersweet baptism for the new four-cylinder Maserati.

The following race, on 14 May, was the Targa Florio for Voiturettes in Palermo, Sicily. It was an all-Maserati event but with no 4CLs as they were still being repaired with an analysis taking place as to what had happened with the engines in Tripoli. The winner was Luigi Villoresi with an old 6CM followed by Piero Taruffi with a similar car from Scuderia Ambrosiana.

Another all-Maserati race was held on 28 May, the Coppa Principessa di Piemonte, in Posillipo, Naples. The works team brought three 4CLs with revised engines and the first privateer to drive one at an event, Johnnie Wakefield, had the fourth. Luigi Villoresi was again the fastest in qualifying, showing the potential of the car, but during the race he could only finish in fourth place after a spin. So, the first victory for the 4CL came from Wakefield, who defeated the Italians by 52 seconds in the 2h 25m race.

On 10 June, the voiturette class took part in a meeting at Donington Park in England for the Nuffield Trophy. Maserati entered two 4CLs for Villoresi and Rocco but they did not appear, leaving the first four places for ERAs and fifth for British privateer Charlie Dodson with a 6CM, the best-placed of three Maseratis.

On 11 June, the Grand Prix de Picardie was held in Peronne, Northern France. Wakefield had the only 4CL and easily dominated the whole weekend, starting from pole position, winning the two races and setting the fastest lap. Local Raymond Sommer with a 6CM finished in second place, two laps behind the winner.

Johnnie Wakefield appeared again in France at the Coupe de la Commission Sportive at Reims-Gueux on 9 July. After Mussolini had issued an order not to race in France, the works Maseratis did not appear and the Alfas stayed home, as did Italian drivers Secondo Cori and Luigi Platé. There were just a dozen cars in the field. Wakefield set the fastest time in qualifying but finished second, two minutes behind Armand Hug with a 4CM.

On 9 July, the works 4CLs were back for the Circuito del Carnaro in Abbazia near Opatija, today in Croatia. It was a 150km race with only Maseratis on the 11-car

The old gives way to the new – Alberto Ascari in the 4CLT (no.34) sweeps past Prince Bira's 4CL on the way to a début victory at the 1948 San Remo Grand Prix, the race that gave the 4CLT its name.
Private collection

20 | Exceptional Cars

The racing career of the 4CL and 4CLT

- The 4CL had made a sensational début at the Tripoli Grand Prix with a streamlined version for Luigi Villoresi which gained pole position from the new Mercedes but, like the other two 4CLs, retired with engine problems in the intense heat.
The Spitzley Zagari Collection

starting grid and the two Officine Maserati-entered 4CLs driven by Villoresi and Cortese finished first and second.

With Mussolini's boycott of French races, no Italians went to the Les Planques circuit in Albi on 16 July. The grid had Maseratis, ERAs, a Bugatti, an MG and an Alta. The ERAs proved fast in qualifying with Arthur Dobson and Raymond Mays sharing the front row of the grid with Johnnie Wakefield's 4CL. For the race, luck was not with the British cars and it was won by Wakefield followed by Reggie Tongue with his 4CL and Prince Bira's ERA. The winner's average speed for the race was an impressive 151km/h (93.8mph).

There were 25 Maseratis at the Coppa Ciano in Livorno, the third voiturette event in July. The race consisted largely of Maseratis, the only exceptions being Platé's Talbot and the four Alfa Corse Alfettas of Farina, Aldrighetti, Biondetti and Pintacuda. The event was divided into two races: the first was the Junior, won by Edoardo Teagno with a Scuderia Torino 6CM, and the second, the Coppa Ciano, saw a duel between Alfa Romeo and Maserati. The front row of the grid was shared by the two Alfas of Farina and Biondetti and the works 4CL of Franco Cortese. Farina led from start to

22 Exceptional Cars

The racing career of the 4CL and 4CLT

Maseratis were ubiquitous in voiturette racing, immediately before and after World War II and an 'all Maserati' starting grid was not unusual. This is the 1939 Coppa Principessa di Piemonte in Napoli, where British privateer Johnnie Wakefield (no. 12) scored the first race win for the 4CL. *The Spitzley Zagari Collection*

finish, taking the chequered flag a lap ahead of second-placed Cortese. Only five cars finished the 2h 30m race and amongst those with problems were the 4CLs of Villoresi, Rocco and Trossi. The little Maserati was proving competitive but was still unreliable.

Voiturettes had become very popular in Italy. On 13 August, the classic Coppa Acerbo was held on the 26km Pescara circuit. As at the Coppa Ciano, the event was divided into two races. The Junior had only Platé's Talbot mixed with 11 Maserati 6CMs; the four-lap race was won by Guido Barbieri. Race 2 was over 14 laps and was dominated by the Alfettas. The Alfas in the first four places, driven by Biondetti, Pintacuda, Farina and Severi, completed the full race distance but the 4CLs of Villoresi and Cortese were not classified as they ran out of fuel one lap before the finish.

For the 1940 season there were only two races for the voiturette class, both organized by the Italians and far from the conflict: the Gran Premio di Tripoli and the Targa Florio in Palermo. The first race was held on 12 May at Mellaha in the Libyan capital. Only Alfas and Maseratis came to the starting line as the Mercedes-Benz team did not show up. Four Alfettas battled against 21 Maseratis including 4CLs and 6CMs.

The racing career of the 4CL and 4CLT

The Scuderia Milano Maserati team at the Nice Grand Prix 1946. From the left, Arialdo Ruggieri (4CL), Philippe Etancelin (6CM 24-valve), Franco Cortese (4CL) and Luigi Villoresi (4CL).
The Spitzley Zagari Collection

In pole position was Farina with the Alfetta. He shared the front row with his team-mates Biondetti and Trossi with Villoresi in a works 4CL in between. Villoresi assumed the lead at the start but it took only one lap for Farina to overtake him. Subsequently Villoresi lost positions to Biondetti and Trossi, finishing in fourth place ahead of Franco Cortese with the other works 4CL.

The Targa Florio on 23 May was an all-Maserati race only for Italian drivers, and was to be the last event for the voiturette class held on European soil until 1945.

The two works 4CLs of Villoresi and Cortese were the fastest in qualifying alongside Giovanni Rocco's car. It was a start-to-finish victory for Villoresi, whilst Cortese and Rocco fought for second place but finished exactly as they started. Ettore Bianco, in his own 4CL, made it 1-2-3-4 for the model.

After the war

Once the war in Europe was over, motor racing was quick to return to liberated France. On 9 September 1945 a series of three races was held in the Bois de Boulogne

The racing career of the 4CL and 4CLT

in Paris. The first was a tribute to Le Mans winner and Resistance fighter Robert Benoist who had been killed by the Gestapo, the second, the Coupe de la Libération, and the third the Coupe des Prisonniers. The grids composed a mix of cars and drivers of different ages and from a variety of places but it was clear that racing was alive. The Coupe de la Libération, for 1.5-3.0 litre cars, was won by Henri Louveau in a Maserati 6CM.

The following spring, on 22 April, the first race of the 1946 season was the Grand Prix Automobile de Nice, on a street circuit. As if nothing had happened in six years, Luigi Villoresi set the pole position time and won the event with a Scuderia Milano Maserati 4CL followed by Raymond Sommer in an Alfa Romeo 308 and another Frenchman, Eugène Chaboud with a Delage Type 135S. In fact, nothing *had* happened to the cars because in that time of austerity no-one could spare the resources to upgrade them.

This was the first of four transitional seasons that would lead to the first Formula 1 World Championship in 1950. Maseratis were prolific in these immediate post-war years, with famous personalities such as Villoresi, Nuvolari and Sommer winning races but also many privateers turning out every time there was an event. Of the competition, Alfa Romeo had the 158, always run by the factory, and the 308 sold to a few private entrants.

Races came thick and fast. On 13 May 1946 Raymond Sommer won in Marseille with a 4CL, then a week later he won the Grand Prix du Forez but this time with a 6CM. With a similar car he won the Coupe René la Bègue on 9 June. On 15 June, Reg Parnell took the Gransden Lodge Trophy with his 4CL. On 14 July, Tazio Nuvolari won the Grand Prix d'Albi in a 4CL that belonged to Enrico Platé. 'Georges Raph' (Raphaël Béthenod) won the Prix des 24 Heures du Mans with a 6CM from the Écurie Naphtra Course. At the Bois de Boulogne on 6 October, Sommer was again victorious with a 4CL, and finally, to close a successful 1946, Giorgio Pelassa won the Gran Premio de Penya Rhin in Pedralbes, Barcelona, driving a Scuderia Milano 4CL. This list shows how strong the Maserati Grand Prix cars were, both in the hands of official or semi-official teams and with privateers.

The experimental T

Over the European winter of 1946, some of the Italian drivers sailed south for the first Argentine Temporada that was to be staged in January 1947. President Juan Domingo Perón was a great fan of motor racing and had asked the Automóvil Club Argentino to organize a series of races for single-seaters to mix the local drivers with pre-war European heroes.

The ACA organized four races: two in Retiro, Buenos Aires, on a street circuit; one at the Parque Independencia in Rosario, in a municipal park; and one at Rafaela, Santa Fe, on the famous dirt track.

The Gran Premio Ciudad de Buenos Aires was held on 9 February and was divided into three races: for Grand Prix cars, Mecánica Nacional Fuerza Libre and Mecánica Nacional Fuerza Limitada. The main show was the Grand Prix race which had the Italian drivers Villoresi, Varzi, Palmieri, Pintacuda, Platé and Bignami racing against the French 'Raph', Brazilian Chico Landi and the locals, Pablo Pessatti, Italo Bizio, Clemar Bucci, 'Pancho' Culligan, Pascual Puopolo and the Gálvez brothers, Juan and Oscar.

The result had seemed a foregone conclusion: Achille Varzi, driving a 3-litre Alfa Romeo 308, would win. But something unexpected happened. In the final laps, Luigi Villoresi, driving a Maserati 4CL for Scuderia Ambrosiana, was leading the race just a few seconds ahead of Varzi who was steadily reducing the advantage, driving the Alfa at a pace only a great champion can achieve. Corrado Filippini, manager of both drivers, informed the leaders there were a couple of laps to go but he was mistaken. The chequered flag went down for Villoresi on lap 50, one lap before either driver expected!

The victory margin was only two seconds and the spectators were amazed. Varzi was not. The Maserati Villoresi drove that day was not a normal 4CL but an experimental car with the familiar four-cylinder 1.5-litre single-stage blown motor in a tubular chassis frame. It was the shape of things to come.

The following week, on 16 February, Varzi would have another chance at the Gran Premio Ciudad de Buenos Aires but was not able to take it as he had to retire very early in the race. Again, Villoresi was the fastest, being

> *Villoresi was driving an experimental car with a tubular chassis frame. It was the shape of things to come*

challenged only by local Oscar Gálvez with his 3.8-litre Alfa Romeo 308 until he retired, and towards the end of the race by another local in an Alfa Romeo 8C-35. Pablo Pessatti finished in second place almost 20 seconds behind the Scuderia Ambrosiana 4CL.

For the Gran Premio Internacional de Rosario held on 1 March, Villoresi set pole position with Varzi's Alfa Romeo second, Pessatti third and Gálvez fourth. The locals were beginning to show their strength. This race had to be Varzi's and so it was. Villoresi's engine stalled on the grid and the car had to be push-started by his mechanics, so he started the chase from last place. On the second lap he was sixth, and on lap six he overtook Gálvez and pushed hard to get on terms with the leader. The last laps saw the the two drivers alternating the lead until lap 49 when Varzi overtook Villoresi for the last time and held the position through the final lap.

The season started in Europe with the Grand Prix de Pau on 7 April won by Nello Pagani in a 4CL. Henri Louveau's car was third but the 4CLs of Sommer and Ruggieri failed to finish.

Meanwhile in South America, after the races in Argentina, drivers and machines went to Brazil for the Grande Premio Cidade Rio De Janeiro on 20 April. The bumpy Gavea circuit was known as *O Trampolin do Diablo*, The Devil's Springboard, and the seven-car race was held in pouring rain. Chico Landi won with the

Maserati 4CLT

The racing career of the 4CL and 4CLT

> *It was evident that the Maserati needed a major upgrade to compete with the Alfas*

Alfa Romeo 308 and Villoresi was second with the 4CL *tubolare* ahead of 'Raph' with the Naphtra Course 6CM.

The next appearance of the 4CLs was at the Jersey Road Race in St. Helier in the Channel Islands. This was a 1-2 for Reg Parnell and Louis Chiron ahead of an army of ERAs.

For the Grand Prix de Marseille on 18 May, Enrico Platé was the best 4CL, in second place behind Eugène Chaboud in a Talbot-Lago. It was not a very good race for the 4CLs with six DNFs for various mechanical reasons. Again in France for the Grand Prix de Nîmes on 1 May, Villoresi harvested another victory, finishing ahead of Chiron's Talbot-Lago and Parnell's 4CL.

The Grand Prix de Suisse on 8 July brought together the Alfettas and 4CLs with some newcomers including a pair of Cisitalia D46s. There were three heats and a final that ended in a 1-2-3 for Alfa Romeo with Wimille, Varzi and Trossi on the podium. Fourth and one lap behind was Raymond Sommer with the 4CL. It was evident that the Maserati was not competitive with the works Alfettas and that a major upgrade was needed to get back to the front line.

The 1947 Grand Prix de Belgique at Spa-Francorchamps on 29 June was also known as the European Grand Prix. This was another parade for the Alfettas: a 1-2-3 for Wimille, Varzi and Trossi sharing a car with Guidotti. The three 4CLs entered for Sommer, Kautz and de Graffenried did not make it to the finish.

In the absence of the works Alfas, the Grand Prix de Reims on 7 July saw a win for the 4CL driven by Christian Kautz, defeating Chiron with the Talbot-Lago. The following week, at the Grand Prix d'Albigeois at Albi, no 4CL could finish the race: Pierre 'Levegh' had a valve problem, 'Raph' also retired with engine trouble, and Villoresi ran out of fuel. Reg Parnell completed only one lap before a piston failed.

The Gran Premio di Bari on 13 July, saw the Alfettas race again without any opposition. Varzi and Sanesi finished first and second, followed by Balestrero and Ziegler with an Alfa Romeo Monza. Privateer Cassano was sixth with a Maserati T26 whilst three 4CLs failed to finish because of mechanical problems.

For the Grand Prix de Nice there were nine 4CLs on the grid, Villoresi's being the fastest. He won the race ahead of local ace Jean-Pierre Wimille with a Simca-Gordini T15. Alberto Ascari was fourth in another 4CL but the other seven did not finish.

On 3 August, Villoresi scored another win at the Grand Prix d'Alsace in France. Yves Giraud-Cabantous and Louis Rosier completed the podium with a pair of Talbot-Lagos. Antonio Branca, Alberto Ascari and Louis Chiron broke their 4CLs. The Grand Prix du Comminges in St. Gaudens in the south of France was won by Louis Chiron in a Talbot-Lago. The best 4CL, in fifth position, was driven by Emmanuel de Graffenried. Alberto Ascari was seventh but Villoresi crashed and had to retire.

The British Empire Trophy was on 21 August in Douglas, Isle of Man. Bob Gerard won with an ERA followed by Peter Whitehead in a similar car and Bob Ansell came third in a 4CL. Prince Bira finished fifth in his 4CL.

On 7 September, the Gran Premio d'Italia was held in Parco Sempione in Milan with 24 cars starting the race. It was an overwhelming win for Alfa Romeo. After three hours of racing, Trossi won followed by Varzi, Sanesi and Alessandro Gaboardi. After the Alfettas came Alberto Ascari with a 4CL, six laps behind the winning car. Five 4CLs did not finish due to mechanical problems.

Back in France, on 21 September, the Grand Prix de l'Automobile Club de France in Lyon was won by Louis Chiron with the Talbot-Lago followed by Henri Louveau in a 4CL. Ascari, 'Raph', de Graffenried and Villoresi all retired with engine problems as did 'Levegh' after crashing his car.

The Swiss organized the Grand Prix de Lausanne on 5 October for 16 cars. Villoresi in a 4CL topped the results one more time, ahead of Jean-Pierre Wimille with a Simca-Gordini and de Graffenried with another 4CL. The last race of 1947 was the Grand Prix du Salon in Montlhéry on 16 November. It was won by Giraud-Cabantous in a Talbot-Lago. The only 4CL to finish the race was Louveau's, in fifth place.

The 1948 season started in the hot summer in Buenos Aires, Argentina, with the Gran Premio del General Juan Perón y de la Ciudad de Buenos Aires held on 17 January. About 75,000 people crowded into Palermo Park to see the two 15-lap heats and the 25-lap final.

The first heat was won by the 4CL of Luigi Villoresi - at this point adopted as one of the local heroes - followed by Varzi in his Alfa Romeo 12C-37, Pascual Puopolo with his 8CL, and, in fourth place, a young (but not that young, at 36) driver called Juan Manuel Fangio with another 4CL.

Nino Farina won the second heat with the big 8CL followed closely by local stock car idol Oscar Gálvez with his 3.8-litre Alfa Romeo 308 and Brazilian Chico Landi in a similar car with a 3-litre engine.

The final made the spectators dream of an Argentinian win as Oscar Gálvez was leading until the eighth lap when he had to retire. The race was won by the experienced Villoresi, followed by Landi, Andrés Fernández in a 6CM, and Arialdo Ruggeri in a Scuderia Milano 4CL. As to the other 4CLs, 'Raph' covered only 21 laps, and Fangio and Platé did not finish.

The Gran Premio Internacional General San Martín, in the circuit of El Torreón in the coastal city of Mar del Plata, was held on 25 January in front of 70,000 spectators. The fastest qualifying lap was set by Villoresi in the 4CL but he had no luck during the race, having to make an unscheduled pit stop and finishing down in ninth place. The race was won by Farina with the 8CL, followed by Varzi's Alfa Romeo and Jean-Pierre Wimille with an Alfa Romeo 308 from the Naphtra Course team. This race also had 4CLs driven by Fangio, Ítalo Bizio, Andrés Fernández, Landi, Cantoni and Ruggeri. Juan Gálvez and Giacomo Palmieri were non-starters.

A week later, on 1 February, on the circuit of the Parque Independencia in Rosario, Gálvez with the Alfa

Exceptional Cars

The racing career of the 4CL and 4CLT

Giuseppe 'Nino' Farina's victory in the 1948 Monaco Grand Prix was the 4CL's last major win before the era of the 4CLT. Farina would be the first Formula 1 World Champion in 1950, driving for Alfa Romeo. *LAT Images*

Romeo and Fangio with a Simca-Gordini were highly motivated, as they had qualified first and second, ahead of the Scuderia Milano 4CLs of Villoresi and Farina. The crowds gathered behind the park's trees to watch the race, started by former driver Carlos Arzani. Gálvez took the lead followed by Farina, Villoresi and Landi. After 25 laps the leading Argentinian came into the pits with transmission problems, and Fangio went ahead for a few laps until he retired with engine failure. The race was won by Wimille, with Landi and Villoresi completing the podium with the 4CL. The other 4CLs of Farina, Ruggeri and Fortunati Firpo retired.

The drivers and machines came back to Buenos Aires for the Gran Premio Dalmiro Varela Castex, also known as Gran Premio Eva Perón, on 14 February. Villoresi with the Scuderia Milano 4CL, set the fastest time on Saturday and fought side-by-side with Gálvez and his Alfa during the race. The Argentinian took the lead after Villoresi made what turned out to be an unnecessary pit stop for fuel and oil. In third place came 'Raph' with the Écurie Naphtra Course 4CL. The two other 4CLs of Firpo and Campos finished in fifth and sixth places.

After the Temporada was over, the European season started in France with the Grand Prix de Pau on 29 March which was dominated by Maserati with a 1-2 for Nello Pagani and Raymond Sommer in 4CLs, followed by a trio of Talbot-Lagos and a Simca-Gordini.

Luigi Villoresi entered the experimental 4CL in the Jersey Road Race but was able to cover just six six laps before the gearbox broke. The 4CLs of Parnell, Bira and Ansell finished 3-4-5 behind the ERA B-type of Bob Gerard and the 6CM of George Abecassis.

For the Grand Prix des Nations in Geneva, Switzerland on 2 May, Farina drove the car that Villoresi had used in the previous race, winning by two minutes from Emmanuel de Graffenried in a 4CL. Argentinian Clemar Bucci, in sixth place with a similar car, was the last finisher.

Maserati 4CLT | 27

The racing career of the 4CL and 4CLT

The first winning drivers with the 4CLT – Alberto Ascari (right) scored the car's début victory in San Remo but Luigi Villoresi (left) was a serial race winner through the second half of 1948. LAT Images

> 'The result could not have been better. Ascari won first time out with the new car'

4CLT debut win at San Remo

By the end of June 1948, Maserati was ready to introduce its new car. This was the 4CLT, later to be known as 4CLT/48 to distiguish it from the modified version of 1950. The announcement was in San Remo, where a Grand Prix was to be held on the 2.62km Ospedaletti street circuit. The result could not have been better: Alberto Ascari won with the new car, with a second example driven by Luigi Villoresi close behind. Clemar Bucci in a 4CL completed the 1-2-3 for Maserati in its homeland. After the victory, the 4CLT also became known as the Maserati San Remo.

The new Maserati was still no match for the Alfetta. The Alfa Romeo team was back for the 4 July Grand Prix de Suisse in Bremgarten and they were first and second in qualifying, two seconds faster than Villoresi. The Swiss race, which had the title of European Grand Prix that year, was dominated by the Alfettas of Carlo Felice Trossi and Jean-Pierre Wimille with Villoresi in the 4CLT in third place, one and a half minutes behind.

The third race for the 4CLT was the Grand Prix de l'Automobile Club de France held on 18 July. It was won by Wimille, but was not a good result for Maserati as the car shared by pre-war star Tazio Nuvolari and Villoresi could only manage seventh place behind three Alfettas and three Talbot-Lagos.

There were no 4CLTs on the grid for the Zandvoort Grand Prix in 7 August but Prince Bira scored a victory

The Grand Prix de Monaco held on 16 May was won by the 4CL *tubolare* driven by Farina after a race of more than three hours. Local Louis Chiron finished in second place with a Talbot-Lago T26. The 4CLs of de Graffenried and Villoresi, sharing the car with Ascari, were third and fifth respectively.

The British Empire Trophy on 25 May in Douglas, Isle of Man, was won by Geoffrey Ansell in an ERA B-Type. Parnell was the best Maserati driver, putting his 4CL in fourth place.

Then came San Remo.

28 | Exceptional Cars

The racing career of the 4CL and 4CLT

When the Alfas were away, the Maseratis made hay. The first RAC Grand Prix at Silverstone in October 1948 saw a 1-2 for the 4CLTs of Villoresi and Ascari. *LAT Images*

for Maserati with his 4CL, winning the second heat and the final. Parnell came in third with another 4CL. The reason for the absence of the new cars in Holland was that the Grand Prix de Comminges at St Gaudens in France was scheduled the same weekend. Villoresi won that race easily in the 4CLT, with a five-minute margin from 'Raph' in a Talbot-Lago T26C. Villoresi also took pole position and the fastest lap of the race.

He was unbeatable again at the Grand Prix de l'Albigeois in Albi on 29 August, taking pole position, winning both races and setting the fastest lap. Philippe Etancelin and Louis Rosier were Villoresi's closest rivals, both with Talbot-Lagos.

Villoresi was at the top of his game but the 4CLT still could not beat the Alfa Romeos. At the Gran Premio d'Italia on 5 September, the 158 of Wimille won by a lap. In qualifying it had been two seconds faster than the Maserati.

Villoresi was able to win the British Grand Prix on 2 October as there were no Alfettas on the grid. Second and close behind was Ascari in a similar 4CLT. Bob Gerard finished third with the ERA B-Type.

The Grand Prix du Salon in Monthléry, held on 10 October was basically a race for the locals as the first three places were taken by Talbot-Lagos and the first five were French drivers. It was won by Rosier, and the best 4CLT was that of Reg Parnell who was able to cover only 42 of the 48 laps.

Maserati 4CLT | 29

The racing career of the 4CL and 4CLT

- Like its predecessors, the 4CLT became a favourite of private teams. Here, in the Maserati factory is a line-up of cars for the 1950 season, including the two owned by the Automóvil Club Argentino, identified by their yellow bonnets.
The Spitzley Zagari Collection

When the Alfettas were present, there was not much opportunity for the *tubolari* Maseratis. The Gran Premio di Monza on 17 October was another clean sweep for Alfa Romeo, who took the first four places. The best Maserati could do was Ascari's fifth place.

Then a new competitor arrived. The race on the Circuito del Garda in Salò, in the north of Italy, on 25 October was won by a Ferrari 125 driven by Giuseppe Farina from Bruno Sterzi with a Ferrari 166 in second place. Villoresi's 4CLT finished third but was only four seconds behind after two and a half hours.

The last race of the international season was the Penya Rhin Grand Prix in Pedralbes, Spain, held on 31 October. Villoresi closed Maserati's 1948 campaign with another win for the 4CLT, followed by Parnell in a similar car. Third and fourth were the Talbot-Lago T26Cs of Chiron and Rosier.

Since the San Remo race in June, the 4CLT had won four times in the hands of Villoresi. While it could not match the works Alfas, it was a promising start for the new model, not only for the official and semi-official teams but also for privateers who wanted to replace their old 4CLs. One such private team was the newly-formed Equipo ACA, from the Automóvil Club Argentino, which had ordered two 4CLTs for the 1949 season.

The Automóvil Club Argentino

- Flying across the world – the ACA contingent, foreground from the left: Alberto Crespo, Juan Manuel Fangio, José Froilán González, Juan Carlos Guzzi (YPF) and Bernardo 'El Mago' Pérez, Fangio's mechanic. *Museo Fangio*

The Automóvil Club Argentino, known as the ACA, was one of the very first organizations of this type in the world. Its origins can be traced back to one person, the sportsman Dalmiro Varela Castex. He was the pioneer who introduced the first automobile to Argentina in 1892. It was only a few years later that, with just 12 cars on the country's roads, the Association was founded to develop not only the use of cars but also motor racing. The first meeting took place on 11 June 1904.

In 1926, the ACA signed an agreement with the Association Internationale des Automobiles Clubs Reconnus (the AIACR, forerunner of the FIA) to recognize it as the sole entity with control of car racing in Argentina. By then there were 110,000 cars in the country and the Club already had 10,000 members.

Among many of the achievements of the ACA was the deal with the local petrol company Yacimientos Petrolíferos Fiscales (YPF) to develop a network of petrol stations that was one of the largest worldwide.

The agreement to sell YPF products was signed in 1936 and the company provided credit to build the new stations. The first opened in 1938 in Córdoba, then Samborombón, Dolores, Pirán and Mar del Plata. By 1939 there were 15 and the ACA had 30,000 members.

The ACA's involvement with racing began in 1910 when it organized the Gran Premio Nacional from Buenos Aires. Later editions of this event went to Córdoba, Bahía Blanca, Rosario and Resistencia. By 1935, the Gran Premio had become an international event of 7,000km in six stages, two of them in Chile. In 1940, it was from Buenos Aires to Lima (Perú), and back.

In 1948 the race was called Gran Premio de la América del Sur, destination Caracas (Venezuela) and covered 9,639km. That race was won by Domingo Marimón. The return race, back to Buenos Aires, had Oscar Alfredo Gálvez as the winner.

The ACA was not only active in organizing and controlling local races but had an essential role in the programme that took local drivers on to the international stage.

The racing career of the 4CL and 4CLT

Carlos P Anesi was the president of the Association from 1940 to 1955 and, with race manager Francisco 'Pancho' Borgonovo, set up a plan to bring international drivers and Grand Prix cars to a series of competitions in Argentina. This was encouraged and supported by President Perón and had the aim of putting European professionals in contact with local drivers who wanted to race internationally. In 1946 the Italian journalist Corrado Filippini was asked to put together a group of drivers and cars to take part in a series of races that would be called Las Temporadas.

The Temporadas would be run from 1947 to 1972, with some interruptions, and included events for Fórmula Libre, Formula 1 and sports cars, including the 1,000 Km de la Ciudad de Buenos Aires as the opening round of the World Sports Car Championship.

After the first Temporada in 1947, the natural next step was to acquire some cars for the local drivers to compete with the Europeans on equal terms. Borgonovo found it very difficult to obtain new cars because of their very high prices, so in organizing the 1948 Temporada, he arranged to rent some cars from the European teams.

The idea of setting up an Argentinian racing team was growing but money was still an issue. For the 1949 Temporada,

● Argentine racing elite - in the group: Benedicto Campos, Héctor Cámpor (Perónist politician), Juan Manuel Fangio, Pascual Puopolo, José Froilán González, Clemar Bucci, Francisco Borgonovo. *Museo Fangio*

● Left, the team's Argentine transporters with a cut-out in the back-board to accommodate the racers' tails. *whitefly.cc*

Exceptional Cars

The racing career of the 4CL and 4CLT

Juan Manuel Fangio started negotiations with Luigi Villoresi to buy his Maserati 4CL and with the Maserati factory to acquire two new 4CLTs. The deal would include the technical assistance of Amadeo Bignami, who was to play an essential role in the team. It was set up as the Equipo Argentino Achille Varzi, named in tribute to the famous driver who had been killed in Switzerland some months before, and made its début at the Gran Premio General Perón, the opening race of the 1949 Temporada with drivers Fangio and Adriano Malusardi.

Several other cars and drivers would soon be added to the ACA stable – they included two Ferrari 166FLs and two Simca-Gordini T15s – and were used alongside the Maseratis in the team's two-year sortie to the classic European events.

● Racers on display at the ACA headquarters after the 1950 European season. Maserati 4CLT 1600 is second in line, with Simca-Gordini in front and Ferrari 166FL and Hudson Super Six behind. Below: While in Europe the team was based at Galliate in Italy at premises owned by the Varzi family. *Museo Fangio/whitefly.cc*

Part 2
The races of 4CLT 1600

Maserati 4CLT serial number 1600 had a 10-year racing career, in Europe running in international events for Grand Prix cars, both Formula 1 and Formula 2, and in Argentina with a Ford engine and many modifications in the Mecánica Nacional Fórmula Libre series.

For its first European season, the Equipo Argentino Achille Varzi came to an agreement with Menotti Varzi, Achille's father, to use his premises in Galliate, some 50km from Milan. The two Maserati 4CLTs – serial numbers 1599 and 1600 – resplendent in the bright blue and yellow Argentinian racing colours were instantly successful in Europe. On the team's first international outing in San Remo on 3 April 1949, Fangio won the race with 1599 and Benedicto Campos finished in fourth place with 1600.

The most important race for 1600 was the Pau Grand Prix in 1950, when Juan Manuel Fangio took victory ahead of Luigi Villoresi with a Ferrari 125GP. The European campaign of the two 4CLTs was remarkable: 1600 scored two Grand Prix victories and 1599 four more, all six driven by Juan Manuel Fangio.

From the start, Fangio was established as the team leader but he was ably supported in the European races by his compatriots Benedicto Campos and José Froilán González. The ACA Maseratis were vital stepping stones to Fangio's works drive for Alfa Romeo and González joining the Ferrari team.

● The Master at the wheel - Juan Manuel Fangio at the 1950 Dutch Grand Prix. Fangio drove 4CLT 1600 in four races in 1950 and won two of them. Sadly, he had to retire in Holland in his last race with the ACA Maseratis.
Grand Prix Library

Chapter 3
1949: ACA's first international season

Unfortunately, no documents have emerged from the archives of the Automóvil Club Argentino to show who owned what in the late-1940s or to understand if the ACA really was the owner behind the names that appear in the Maserati and Ferrari archives. In those, the name Giuseppe Vianini is sometimes listed as the first owner, and also as the Italian link for the Argentinians purchasing cars. Back then it was not easy to move money from one continent to another, so people found weird ways to transfer funds. There is also a company named AICAR, Franco Cornacchia's Agenzia Internazionale Commerciale Auto Ricambi, that appears in connection with cars that later came to Argentina.

When it comes to the ACA Maseratis, there is still no public document that shows who put up the money for the cars or, indeed, the whole operation. In his book *Fangio Conquers Europe*, Guillermo Sánchez, now known as Guillermo Sánchez Bouchard, says that Fangio raised the funds for one 4CLT and Villoresi's used 4CL, and Adriano Malusardi brought the money to buy 1600. Malusardi drove 1600 in its first three races but it is not known if he actually paid for the car as he died in a racing accident early in 1949.

The ACA's intentions for the International Temporadas was to gather as many drivers and cars as possible so these races were run under Fórmula Libre rules. This is why they had a strange mix of cars, big and small, pre-war and post-war, and with four-, six-, eight- or twelve-cylinder engines.

The Temporada

29 January 1949. Trofeo General Perón. Palermo, Buenos Aires, Argentina. FL
#4 Adriano Malusardi 7th
The début of 4CLT 1600 took place under sad circumstances. During practice for the race, the French driver Jean-Pierre Wimille lost control of his Simca-Gordini, it flipped over and he lost his life. Everyone was shocked, but the competition had to go on. The grid was dominated by Maseratis in the first 10 positions, and for the race the Alfa Romeo 8C 308 of Oscar Alfredo Gálvez was the only non-Maserati amongst the first eight cars. Though Malusardi was recorded in seventh position he had to retire after 25 laps. Alberto Ascari was the winner with another 4CLT.

6 February 1949. Premio María Eva Duarte de Perón. Palermo, Buenos Aires, Argentina. FL
#4 Adriano Malusardi 4th
There were two races on that day. The first one for Mecánica Nacional was named after the late Jean-Pierre Wimille and was won by Juan Manuel Fangio with a Volpi-Chevrolet. The second one for the international drivers and machines was also won by a local, Oscar Alfredo Gálvez with an old Alfa Romeo 8C 308, taking advantage of heavy rain. Adriano Malusardi came home in fourth place, three laps behind the winner.

San Remo Grand Prix 1949 – scene of the 4CLT's début victory the year before – the first European race for the ACA cars, and Fangio's first win in Europe. Here Fangio in 1599 leads Campos in 1600 on the opening lap. Campos was to finish a creditable fourth.
whitefly.cc

Exceptional Cars

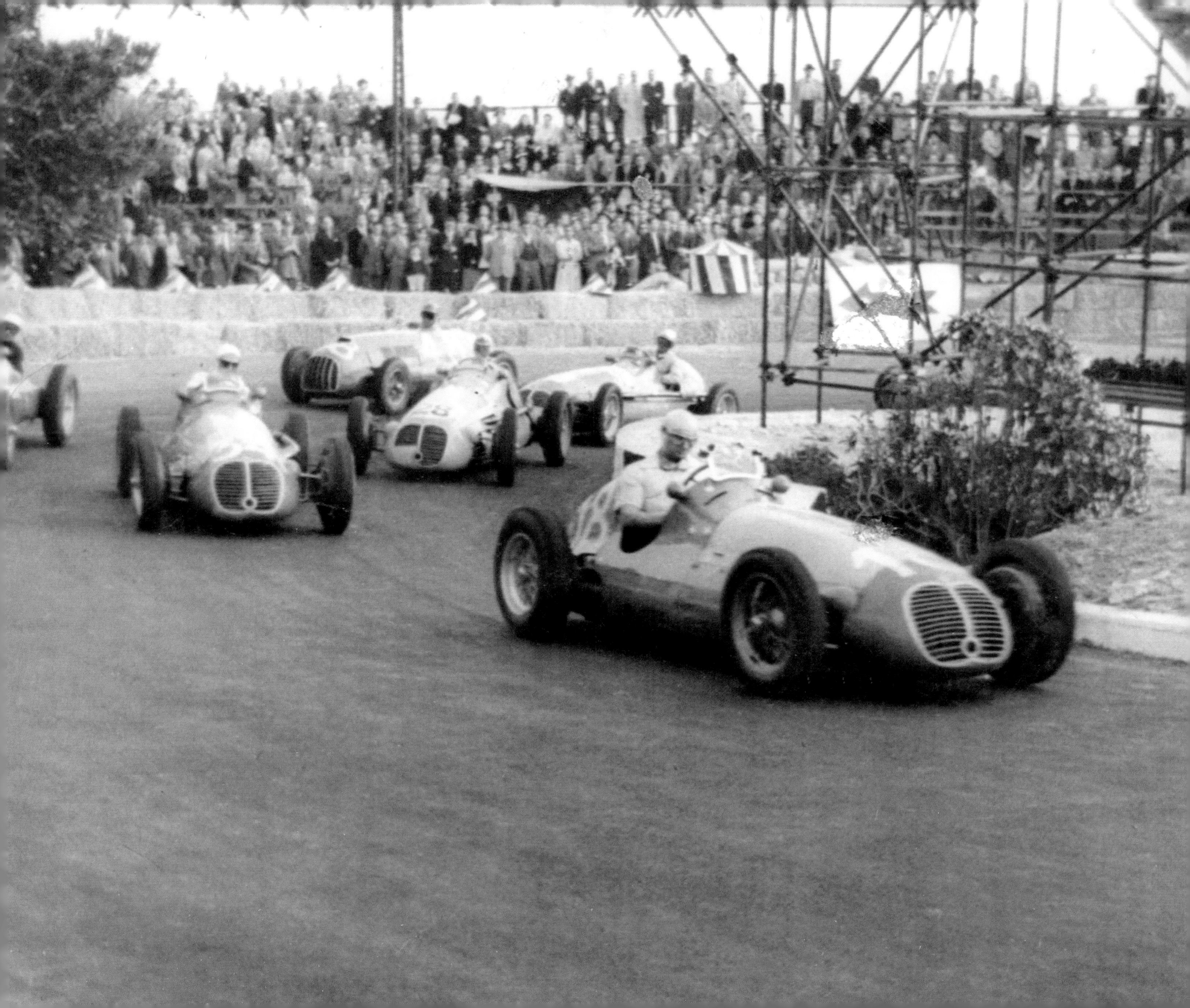

1949: ACA's first international season

The Trofeo General Perón, opening race of the 1949 Temporada, was the first race for the ACA Maserati 4CLTs and 1600 was driven by Adriano Malusardi. Although the car retired with mechanical problems, it was classified seventh.
whitefly.cc

13 February 1949. Gran Premio Ciudad de Rosario. Parque Independencia, Rosario, Argentina. Copa Acción San Lorenzo FL
#4 Adriano Malusardi. DNF
Nino Farina achieved one of the first victories for Ferrari outside Italy at the wheel of a 125C F1 which was probably equipped with a 2-litre engine, as it was in Palermo. Malusardi had to retire from what would be his last race as two weeks later he was to lose his life in Mar del Plata driving his Alfa Romeo Tipo B.

27 February 1949. Premio Ciudad de Mar del Plata 1949
#36 Emilio Karstulovich. DNS
For some reason Malusardi drove his Alfa Romeo Tipo B and Emilio Karstulovich was entered with 4CLT 1600, but it did not start the race.

The European campaign

After the Temporada in 1949 the cars and drivers moved to Europe. The Argentine team had its base in Galliate, Italy, at a warehouse rented by the Automóvil Club Argentino from Menotti Varzi, the father of Achille Varzi who had lost his life testing an Alfetta in Switzerland on 1 July 1948. There, the team had the two 4CLTs, 1599 and 1600, and other cars including a 4CL, two Ferrari 166FLs, and a pair of Simca-Gordinis.

Juan-Manuel Fangio was joined in the team by Benedicto Campos, who was allocated 1600 for the 1949 European season.

3 April 1949. Gran Premio di San Remo.
#34 Benedicto Campos. 4th
The Equipo ACA opened the season at the San Remo race

38 | Exceptional Cars

1949: ACA's first international season

in Italy where the previous year the 4CLT made its début with a victory in the hands of Alberto Ascari. Fangio won the three-hour race with 1599, covering 90 laps, and Campos finished in fourth place with 89 laps, behind the 4CLTs of Bira and Emmanuel de Graffenried. The 2-litre Ferraris of Felice Bonetto and Giovanni Bracco followed Campos home.

18 April 1949. Grand Prix de Pau.
#6 Benedicto Campos. 3rd
After the victory of Juan Manuel Fangio in San Remo, he was starting to be considered an exotic phenomenon, but it was with the win at Pau, after three and a half hours of exhausting competition, that the blue-eyed Argentinian driver began to be taken seriously. The 4CLT he drove was the same winning car and Campos in 1600 backed him up with third place behind de Graffenried, covering only one lap less than his team-mate.

7 May 1949. Grand Prix de Rousillon.
#6 Benedicto Campos. 3rd
After three wins in a row, including one in Mar del Plata, the last race of Temporada, everyone was looking at Fangio, who was very focused on winning a fourth. The Grand Prix was over 50 laps divided into two 25-lap heats, the result being on the aggregate time from the two races. The first race was a battle between Fangio and Villoresi until the Italian had to go into the pits with fuel pump problems. The second one was won by Bira and the combined classification gave Fangio overall honours. Campos, once again driving 4CLT 1600, came in third.

Brothers in arms – Benedicto Campos and Juan Manuel Fangio arrived in Europe as team-mates in the two ACA 4CLTs. Campos was allocated 1600 for the entire European season. His best results were third places – at Pau and Rousillon – but at the Belgian Grand Prix (right) he had to retire with engine failure. *Héctor Diaz*

Maserati 4CLT

1949: ACA's first international season

1949: ACA's first international season

- Pau Grand Prix 1949 saw the second successive win for Fangio (no.4), who was followed by Campos (no.6) in third place. With no works Alfa Romeos present, Maserati 4CLTs were the class of the field. *Museo Fangio*

- The ACA Maseratis and their Argentine drivers created great interest wherever they appeared. This was the scene in the paddock at Reims for the French Grand Prix with 1599, Fangio's car, the centre of attention. *LAT Images*

19 June 1949. Grand Prix de Belgique.
#10 Benedicto Campos. DNF (engine)
This was a bad day for the Equipo ACA as both of its Maserati 4CLTs had to retire with engine troubles. Fangio lasted only one lap and Campos, after battling for fifth place, saw his chances come to an end when the oil pump broke on lap 21 of 25. Victory went to Louis Rosier with a Talbot-Lago T26C followed by the Ferraris of Villoresi and Ascari.

10 July 1949. Grand Prix d'Albi.
#10 Benedicto Campos. DNF (driver illness)
Fangio won again: his fourth victory in five races in Europe. There were five 4CLTs in the first nine places which showed how competitive the Italian racer had become. It was another bad race for Campos and 1600 as he had to retire with heat exhaustion and asphyxiation from exhaust gases.

17 July 1949. Grand Prix de France.
#36 Benedicto Campos. DNF (valves)
This event was the third DNF of four in a row for Campos and 4CLT 1600. The first part of the race was an exciting battle between Fangio and Campos. The *balcarceño* was leading until he stopped for fuel and afterwards retired with a broken throttle. Campos led the race for a few

Maserati 4CLT

1949: ACA's first international season

laps but a damaged valve prevented him from finishing. It was an acclaimed victory for Monégasque driver Louis Chiron with a Talbot-Lago T26C.

11 September 1949. Gran Premio de Italia.
#2 Benedicto Campos. DNF (engine)
Campos ran once again in 1600 and was the only Argentinian entered for the race. In practice he set the fifth fastest time behind Ascari, Villoresi, Farina and Rosier. He had competitive race pace but had to retire after 55 laps out of 80 with a broken connecting rod. This was his last appearance in Europe before going back to Argentina to race local stock cars.

Interviews from the time suggest that Campos left the team because he never wanted to have to thank General Perón publicly for the opportunity of driving a car from the Automóvil Club Argentino. He said that he saw himself as a sportsman and did not want to get involved in politics.

• The field streaks away at the start of the French Grand Prix at Reims. Fangio and Campos both held the lead in this race but the eventual winner was Chiron's Talbot-Lago. *LAT Images*

Reims would go down • as one of the best performances by Benedicto Campos, who led the French Grand Prix in 1600 until side-lined with engine trouble. *Héctor Diaz*

42 | Exceptional Cars

1949: ACA's first international season

1949: ACA's first international season

- Two Ferraris storm away in the lead at the Italian Grand Prix, won by Alberto Ascari. Campos in 1600 was the sole ACA entry in this race but once again was forced to retire with engine trouble. *LAT Images*

- High-speed farewell - Monza was to be the last European Grand Prix for Benedicto Campos. *LAT Images*

- The Automóvil Club Argentino had a successful first season in Europe, with Benedicto Campos (left) a congenial team-mate for future World Champion Juan Manuel Fangio. *Museo Fangio*

44 | Exceptional Cars

1949: ACA's first international season

Maserati 4CLT 45

1949: ACA's first international season

Adriano Domingo Malusardi
The first to race 4CLT 1600

Pocholo Malusardi was born in 1909 in the city of Buenos Aires, gaining the nickname *El pibe de Barracas* (the kid from Barracas), because he was from that neighbourhood in the south of the city.

The records are not entirely clear but it seems that he made his first appereance in racing driving a Ford on 3 October 1934 in an international race held in Gavea, for the II Grande Prêmio da Ciudade do Rio de Janeiro. Although his driving made a good impression, the car was not competitive.

Three years later, Malusardi finished fourth in a race at the circuit of San Isidro in Buenos Aires featuring local heroes Carlos Arzani and Ricardo Nasi where all the front-runners were in Alfa Romeos. He collected a win in 1937 at Esperanza in Santa Fe and in 1942 at El Plumerillo in Mendoza.

He became well-known when he bought an Alfa Romeo Tipo B from local ace, Ford stock car driver Juan Gálvez. 'Pocholo' drove the Alfa for the first time in a race in March 1948 at the 100 Millas Playas de Necochea in the province of Buenos Aires where he came home in second place. Then in June he won the Premio Colonizadores, in Esperanza.

His performances gained him the seat of the ACA Maserati 4CLT 1600 for the first races of the 1949 Temporada, as team mate to Juan Manuel Fangio. Malusardi had the opportunity to drive the car when it was brand new in the two events held in Buenos Aires and the one in Rosario.

On 26 February 1949, at the Mar del Plata race at El Torreón street circuit beside the Atlantic, he drove his Alfa Romeo for the last time. On a very slow left-hand turn he went too wide and touched the kerb with the rear right wheel, flipping the car which immediately caught fire, killing Malusardi. That was a big shock for a very popular sport in Argentina and would lead, after other fatalities, to the construction of the Autódromo de Buenos Aires a few years later.

- The career of Adriano Malusardi, a successful racer in Argentina, was tragically cut short after the first three races for 4CLT 1600 in the 1949 Temporada. *whitefly.cc*

Exceptional Cars

Benedicto Campos
Fangio's team-mate in Europe, 1949

• Campos was nominated by the ACA to drive alongside Fangio in the team that went to Europe in 1949 but at the end of the season returned home to race in Argentina. *LAT Images*

Born in Necochea, in the province of Buenos Aires, Benedicto Campos was a single-seater and stock car driver. He made his début at the age of 23 in Benito Juárez driving a Dodge which later had an engine transplant with a more powerful Ford unit and with which he started his successful career. In 1938 he won his first race, the Playas de Necochea at the wheel of a Ford T which he had bought from a local polo player.

Campos continued with stock cars throughout the 1940s – with some interruption during the war years – and then bought a midget race car he prepared himself and christened 'Betty' after his daughter's nickname. He won the Gran Premio Ciudad de Coronel Pringles defeating three already big names: Juan Manuel Fangio, Oscar Alfredo Gálvez and Pable Gulle.

After a very good 1948 season, he was invited by Fangio to join the ACA team that would race in the European season for single-seaters. His campaign in 1949 would consist of a total of eight races with the Maserati 4CLT and a Simca-Gordini T15. With 4CLT 1600 he harvested a fourth and two third places and four retirements. As recounted earlier this chapter, Campos left the ACA team at the end of the year, feeling that, as a sportsman, he did not want to be politicized by association with General Perón.

Nevertheless, on his return to Argentina, he drove one of the ACA Ferrari 166FLs in Fórmula Libre in 1950. He also used his Cadillac 16 in Mecánica Nacional Fuerza Libre and won the championship.

Campos retired from racing in 1951 to devote more time to his agricultural business. He died in 1972, at the age of 59, of a heart attack while driving his car on a business trip near Chascomús in the province of Buenos Aires.

1949: ACA's first international season

Juan Manuel Fangio
On the way to five World Championships

Juan Manuel Fangio's international career accelerated with the ACA Maseratis but from 1950 onwards he was to drive for other teams, winning the World Championship with Alfa Romeo, Maserati, Mercedes and Ferrari. His amazing career even included a few races with the fearsome BRM V16 shown here. *Popperfoto/Getty Images*

Since he was a kid in Balcarce, in the province of Buenos Aires, Juan Manuel Fangio was known as *El Chueco* (bow-legged). Born in 1911, Juan Manuel was the fourth child of Italian immigrants, Loreto Fangio and Herminia D'Eramo.

From a very early age he knew how to drive cars and tractors, and understood the language of machines. At the age of nine he started working after school as a blacksmith, repairing carriages to help his family, and when he was only 11 he moved to a mechanical workshop. In the early 1920s when he joined Raimundo Carlini's Rugby dealership, Carlini offered Fangio the chance to prepare a car and for them to go racing together.

His own first car was an Overland, acquired at the age of 16 as payment for his work, but cars were not his only passion. Soccer was something that really motivated him so he started playing for Club Rivadavia and even reached the Balcarce team. He also practised boxing as a hobby.

Before World War II, stock cars were the best way for enthusiasts in Argentina to get into motor racing. Although money was always needed, stock car racing was more based on effort and perseverance than economic resources. Local drivers and tuners would raise funds from a *peña* - people from the town organizing a raffle or just throwing some money into a basket.

Fangio's début was a collective effort. On 25 October 1936, with the help of some friends, he borrowed a 1929 Ford A taxi-cab from a client and headed for a race at Benito Juárez, about 170km from Balcarce. He qualified in seventh place and in the race he was third two laps from the end when the engine ran out of oil and he had to retire. His second race was in December that year, again with a Ford A but with no luck as he was disqualified for a late arrival at the start.

In March 1937 he competed for the first and only time in his hometown Balcarce at the wheel of an eight-cylinder Buick. The local press instantly identified him as a promising youngster but the bad luck was still with him as he had to retire with a gearbox problem.

On 27 March 1938 Fangio made his official début on the road circuit at Necochea at the wheel of a Ford V8, with riding mechanic 'Pichón' Bianculli. It was a Fuerza Libre race under the jurisdiction of the Automóvil Club Argentino. He was fifth fastest of 26 contenders in the rain, surprising everybody because of his limited experience and capability of his car. In the race he finished seventh, one lap behind the winner, Carlos Arzani in his almost unbeatable Alfa Romeo 8C-35.

Exceptional Cars

1949: ACA's first international season

His next race was his first in Turismo Carretera, Argentina's long-distance road races. The Gran Premio Argentino de Carretera was held from 18 to 30 October 1938 and he competed with Luis Finocchietti, also from Balcarce. Although Fangio was not the main driver, he took the wheel for much of the race. They finished seventh.

On Sunday 13 November he was in eighth position at the Circuito de Tres Arroyos with the Ford V8 and Bianculli when the race was stopped because of a terrible accident in which Plácido Ruiz, Fermín Martín, Miguel Zatuszek and a spectator lost their lives.

His first race in 1939 was in La Plata at the Circuito El Bosque on 7 May, driving his Ford V8 for the last time. Joining him this time was Héctor Tieri, a mechanic from his workshop. Because of their limited budget, they drove from Balcarce to La Plata in the racing car, covering about 370 km. The race was again won by Carlos Arzani in his Alfa Romeo and Fangio finished eighth in the final.

The Gran Premio Argentino was one of the most important Turismo Carretera races and on 19 October 1939 Fangio was back, this time as the prime driver, with Héctor Tieri as co-driver, in a black Chevrolet that had been bought with the help of his friends from Balcarce. At half-distance in Concordia, when he was in in 22nd place, the race was stopped because of heavy rain. It re-started from Córdoba, re-named Gran Premio Extraordinario. Soon the rookie was ahead of the official Chevrolet team car and achieved his first stage win, which put him on top of the leader board, but then an accident dropped him to fifth place.

His first win in Turismo Carretera was in a gruelling 9,500-km competition that started in Buenos Aires, went to Lima, Perú and came back to where it started. The car was a green 1940 Chevrolet that had been first prize in a raffle. With the cash he won, he was able to buy the car and inject some money into his business. At the end of the season he was Turismo Carretera champion, beating the Gálvez brothers' Ford. It was the beginning of a local rivalry that still exists: Ford versus Chevrolet.

In June 1940 Fangio scored an international win at the Gran Premio Getulio Vargas in Brazil, defeating Oscar Gálvez. In December, he won the Mil Millas Argentinas and was crowned Turismo Carretera champion for the second time. By then, Fangio was on the cover of the magazines like *El Gráfico* and his popularity was growing rapidly. Anselmo Aieta dedicated a tango to him called 'Fangio'.

The following year there were only a few races because of the war. Fangio finished 10th in the Gran Premio del Sur and then won the Mar y Sierras race, in both cases driving his green Chevrolet coupé.

Fangio had set up his own workshop in Balcarce and in 1940 it had been expanded by buying the property

● A young Fangio at the wheel of a Ford Model A Special at the Circuito de González Chávez in Buenos Aires in December 1936.
Museo Fangio

Maserati 4CLT | 49

1949: ACA's first international season

next door. He set up the company Fangio, Duffard and Co. with his friend and partner José Duffard, and his younger brother Rubén Renato, known as 'Toto', joined the team. In 1943, with no races, Fangio focused on his business. Wartime provided some unusual opportunities. He joined Héctor Barragán and bought trucks and trailers around the country, just for the wheels that were very difficult to obtain.

In 1946 motor racing resumed and Fangio was back in action driving Ford Ts lent by two of his friends in the dirt tracks of Morón and Tandil.

Dictator Juan Perón was a fan of motor racing so as soon as he could he gave the order to organize a series of races that were known as La Temporada Internacional. For the first one in the hot summer of 1947 he invited the European masters Villoresi, Palmieri, Pintacuda, 'Raph' and Varzi, who mixed with locals Oscar Gálvez and Brazilian Chico Landi with their private Alfa Romeo 308s.

Clemar Bucci, who won the Gran Premio Ciudad de Buenos Aires for Mecánica Nacional Fuerza Libre cars,

● This Chevrolet coupé was Fangio's stock car for two of the gruelling South American road races in 1939. It was a learning time for the mechanic who was becoming a race driver. *Museo Fangio*

● Post-war, Fangio gained single-seater experience – and some useful results – with this Chevrolet Special. Later, as part of Escudería JM Fangio, it was driven by his protégé Onofre Marimón. *whitefly.cc*

50 | Exceptional Cars

1949: ACA's first international season

described this as a turning point for him and the other drivers who had the opportunity to see the Europeans' driving skills and techniques. That day Fangio drove his Chevrolet special nicknamed 'La Negrita' (because it was painted black) to third place, only a few seconds behind the winner.

For the first day of March the whole circus moved to Rosario, a city 300km north of Buenos Aires for the Gran Premio Copa Acción de San Lorenzo. The race for Fuerza Libre cars was won by Fangio in his Chevrolet so he was allowed to start the race for the Grand Prix cars with 'La Negrita', marking his international début in a race for single-seaters. The Gran Premio Ciudad de Rosario was won by Achille Varzi with the Écurie Naphtra Course Alfa Romeo 308 and Fangio finished in sixth place. In Rosario Fangio also won the Premio Ciudad de Buenos Aires for Mecánica Nacional, closing an amazing performance through the whole Temporada.

To replace 'La Negrita', Fangio bought another Mecánica Nacional car that had a Volpi chassis which was much more developed than its competitors. It had a Rickenbaker engine that soon was replaced by a six-cylinder Chevrolet. With this car, that today sits besides 'La Negrita' in the Fangio museum in Balcarce, he won the Gran Premio Ciudad de Montevideo in Uruguay in August and the Gran Premio Primavera in Mar del Plata in September. From then on, always prepared by his brother Toto, 'La Petisa' (because it was low) and Fangio won almost every race of the dozen he started.

For the 1948 Temporada he made his début in a Grand Prix car driving a Maserati 4CL from the Écurie Naphtra Course. He retired in Buenos Aires and finished fifth in Mar del Plata. For the race in Rosario Fangio drove a Simca-Gordini from the ACA but had to retire after qualifying in second place. Back in Buenos Aires for another race, Fangio again drove the French car but failed to make the finish.

Some days later, he won the Vuelta de Pringles in Entre Ríos in his red Turismo Carretera Chevrolet and had three wins in Mecánica Nacional driving his Volpi-Chevrolet: the Premio Otoño in Palermo, the 100 Millas Playas de Necochea and the Premio Ciudad de Mercedes in Uruguay.

In July Fangio and other drivers travelled to Europe where he was invited to drive at Reims by Amédée Gordini. It was his European début in Grand Prix racing.

Back in Argentina he closed the season at the Gran Premio de América del Sur, a very tough and challenging Turismo Carretera race that went from Buenos Aires to Caracas. This event would haunt Fangio forever. On the seventh stage in Lima, Perú, he rolled the car and his co-driver Daniel Urrutia lost his life.

In January 1949 he finished second at the Mil Millas Argentinas with his Chevrolet coupé and he had his first race in one of the two brand new Maserati 4CLTs that the ACA had brought to the Gran Premio Presidente Perón, the opening event of the Temporada Internacional. The race was won by Alberto Ascari in a Scuderai Ambrosiana 4CLT and Fangio, aboard the ACA 4CLT 1599, was fourth.

The first race for Fangio in a Maserati 4CLT was the 42nd of his career. To get to that point he had driven in many different types of cars and was already regarded as a serious contender in South America. The ACA Maseratis were – perhaps more than any other cars – the springboard to a fantastic international career that was to bring no less than five World Championships.

Juan Manuel Fangio, who many regard as the greatest racing driver of all time, retired from race driving in 1958. He died, aged 84, on 17 July 1995.

The end of an era – Fangio, appropriately driving a Maserati (250F), gives way to Stirling Moss' Vanwall in the 1958 French Grand Prix, his last race. LAT Images

Chapter 4
1950: Fangio scores 1600's greatest victory

For the 1950 season the two 4CLTs received an update at the Maserati factory that included the '4CLT/50' modifications, the most recognizable being the oil tank fitted at the front right with the cap being visible from the outside. Whilst 1599 was driven in the Temporada Argentina by González at Mar del Plata and Rosario, 1600 remained unused while ACA entered its two Ferrari 166s.

10 April 1950. Grand Prix de Pau.
#10 Juan Manuel Fangio. 1st
The most important race in the history of 4CLT 1600 was the victory at Pau in 1950 in the hands of Juan Manuel Fangio. It was the first time Fangio had driven 1600 and was to be first of successive wins, giving him a 100 per cent success record with this car.

El Chueco dominated during the whole weekend. He set the fastest time in qualifying, covering a lap in 1m 43.1s. Very close behind was Villoresi with a Ferrari 125C at 1m 43.4s and Sommer with another Ferrari (1m 44.5s).

At the start, Fangio lost the lead to Villoresi and Sommer. Behind him was Froilán González with the other ACA Maserati 4CLT (1599). The three leaders were soon in a race on their own. On the fourth lap Sommer overtook Villoresi at the Foch corner. Soon Fangio took advantage of the situation and moved into second place just in front of the grandstands. Then Fangio started to attack Sommer, trying to get the lead at Ave. Leon Say without success; Sommer was not going to give up easily. It was not until lap 15 that the scoreboard changed with Fangio holding the lead, which he was to keep for the rest of the race.

After two laps in the lead, Fangio set a new lap record at 1m 42.8s, three-tenths faster than his qualifying speed. It was a very tough race for everyone, especially for González who had to retire when the differential of his Maserati failed, leaving fourth place to Rosier's Talbot-Lago.

With Fangio out on his own in the lead, the battle for second place was between Sommer and Villoresi. The French driver had clutch problems and had to give up the second place to the Italian.

By lap 40, only Villoresi, Sommer and Rosier were on the same lap as Fangio but with no chance of catching him. Way behind came the French Talbot and Simca-Gordinis of Manzon, 'Levegh', Trintignant and Pozzi.

On lap 50, Fangio came into the pits for fuel, a stop of 55 seconds which was a poor time compared with the 33 seconds Villoresi spent in the Scuderia Ferrari pit, but Fangio's advantage was such that he regained the track without losing the lead.

By the end of the race, after 3 h 14m covering 110 laps, the advantage over Villoresi was 30 seconds and more than a minute over Rosier.

At the finish, Fangio was widely acclaimed and immediately interviewed by the Sojit brothers, two reporters from Argentina who were broadcasting the event for the South American fans.

Fangio was no longer a promising newcomer. Instead he was looking like a future champion.

Renowned artist Michael Turner captures 4CLT 1600's finest moment: the 1950 Pau Grand Prix when Juan Manuel Fangio beat Luigi Villoresi in the Ferrari 166 by 30 seconds. The Talbot-Lago of third place Louis Rosier is shown in the background on this picturesque street circuit.
Courtesy of Michael Turner

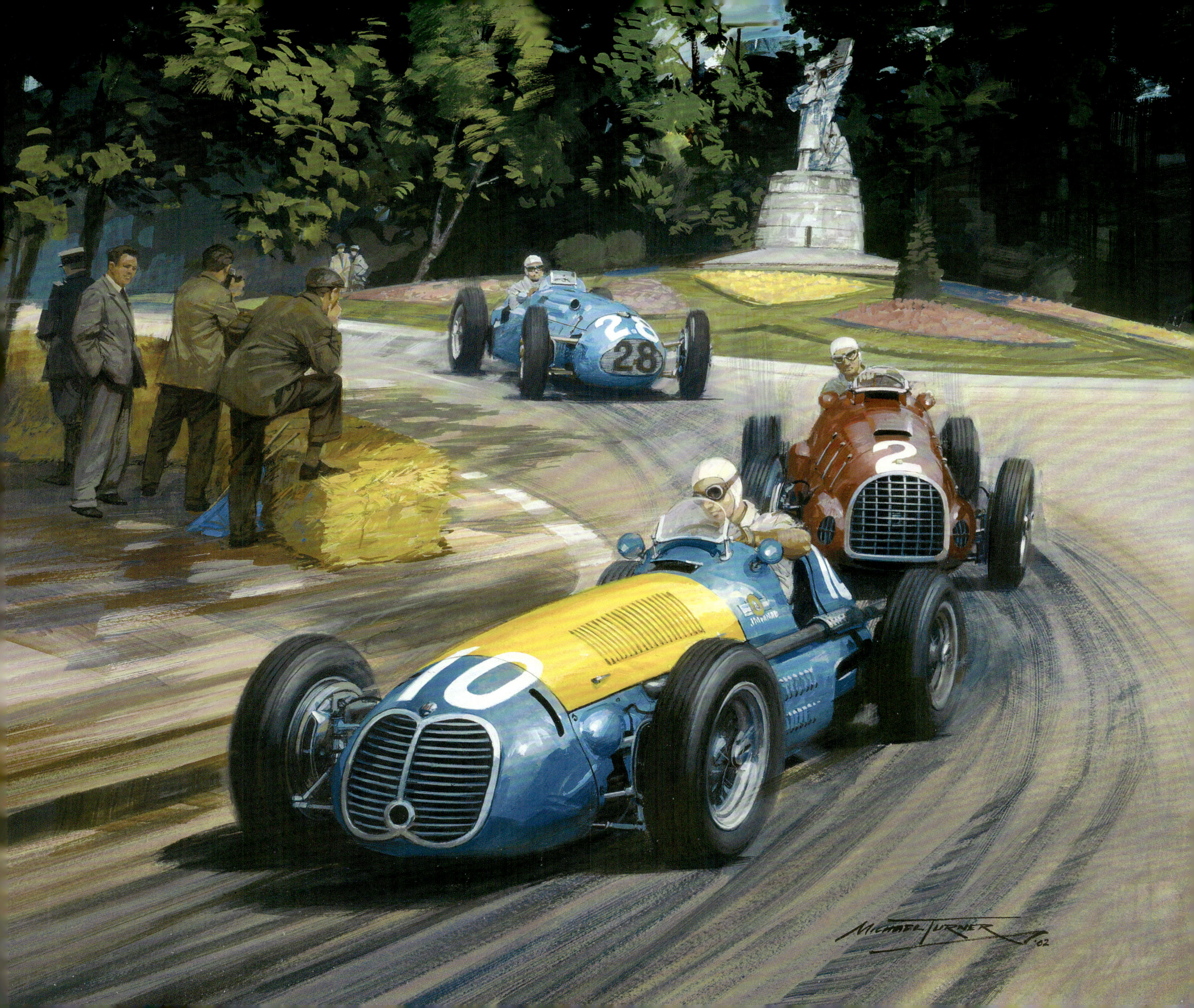
28
2
10
MICHAEL TURNER '02

1950: Fangio scores 1600's greatest victory

Fangio's win at Pau repeated his 1949 success in this European season opener. The 1950 race was the first time that he had driven 1600.
Keystone-Gamma /Getty Images

The battle of the race was between Fangio in 1600 and the Ferrari 166 of Villoresi but Fangio led from lap 15, with Villoresi closing the gap towards the end of the race after refuelling stops.
Keystone-Gamma /Getty Images

Congratulations for the winner after the finish at Pau, with team-mate Froilán González at the forefront. It was a tough race and the sister car of González retired after the differential failed.
Keystone-Gamma /Getty Images

54 | Exceptional Cars

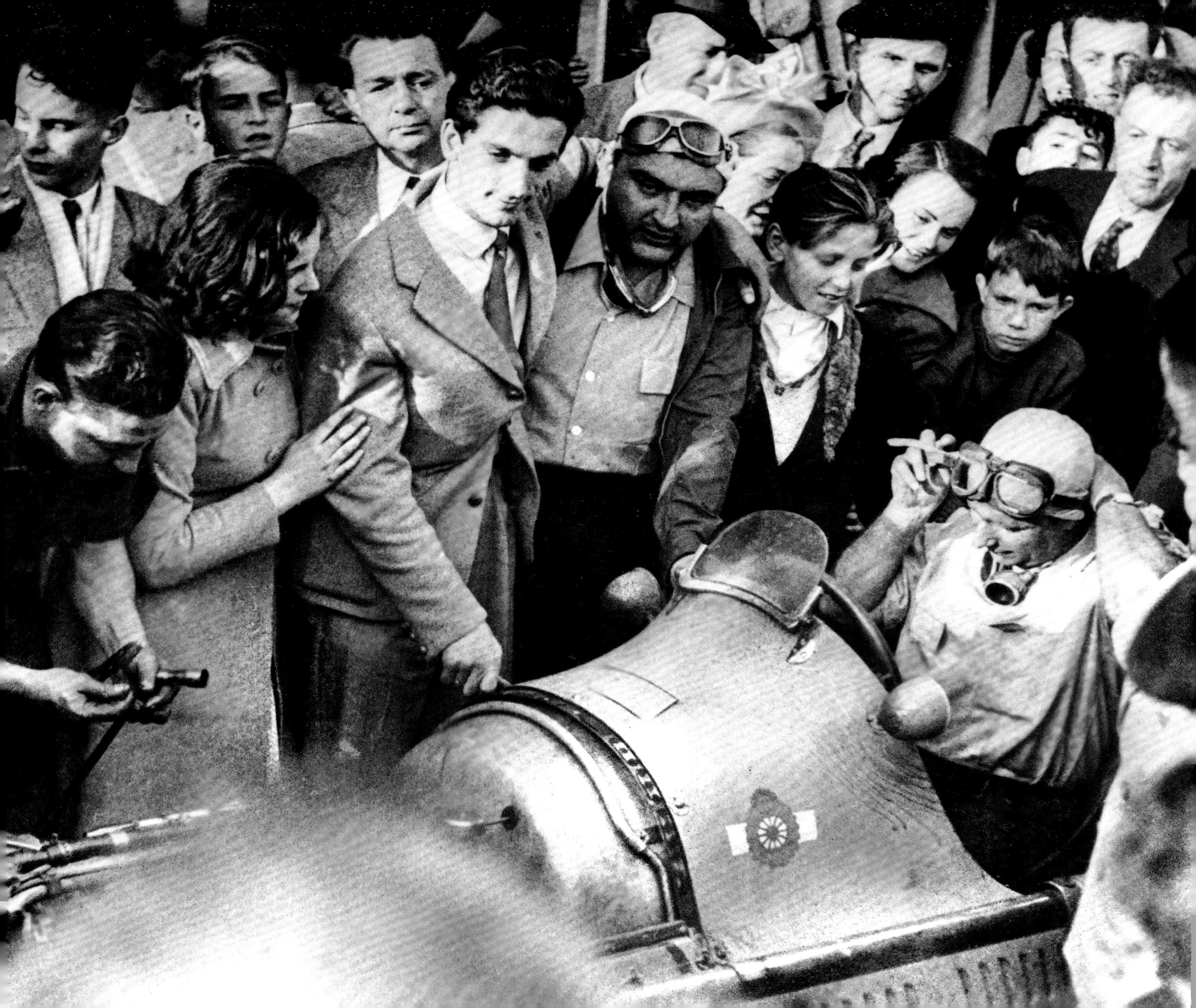

1950: Fangio scores 1600's greatest victory

Commemorative photo of Fangio after his second win with 1600, the Coupe Internationale Automobile des Remparts at Angoulême, a Formula 2 race for which the car was fitted with a naturally-aspirated 2-litre engine.
Ton Blankvoort collection

11 June 1950 Coupe Internationale Automobile des Remparts. Angoulême. F2
#10 Juan Manuel Fangio. 1st
The second victory in a row for Fangio with 1600 but this time the car was fitted with an experimental 2-litre naturally-aspirated engine for the Formula 2 rules. Mechanics led by Amedeo Bignami fitted the six-cylinder engine with three carburettors into the Grand Prix chassis frame. The only notable modification was to the radiator, to fit the crank to start the engine that was positioned a few centimetres higher than on the four-cylinder. This meant that the crank hole was oval rather than round as it had to serve for both engines.

The Angoulême race, known as the Grand Prix de Remparts, was run under the new 2-litre Formula 2 regulations. The circuit was in the middle of the city, and the start was just beside the Cathédrale Saint-Pierre d'Angoulême, a Romanesque cathedral built in the 12th century. It was a slow circuit with many bends and only short straights.

Froilán González was returning to competition after injuries at the Monaco Grand Prix where, driving one of the ACA's Ferrari 166s, he suffered burns to one of his arms. The team, worried about González's condition, entered Roberto 'Bitito' Mieres as a back-up driver.

During qualifying Fangio was fastest, followed by Maurice Trintignant with a small and nimble Simca-Gordini, showing that power was not necessarily an advantage for this 'round the houses' race.

At the start Fangio had problems with the gearbox and lost many places, so he had to drive from the back, fighting not only with the other drivers but also with tremendous heat. On lap 20 Fangio overtook González and took the lead which he would keep until the end of the race.

Interviewed by journalist Roberto Carozzo for one of his biographies, Fangio said: 'That day I thought I was going to die because of the heat. At the start the gearbox jumped into neutral and I was overtaken before I could reconnect the first gear. After that I drove like a maniac until I took the lead. When I got there I was finished, completely exhausted. I thought I was near the finish when I was informed by my team that I was 110 laps away! The tension during the first laps was so high that after that I thought I was not going to make it. It was a circuit that could be done in about a minute, and it was a 130-lap race with a suffocating heat. The only air I could get was by folding down the aeroscreen of the Maserati. Fortunately someone refreshed me in one of the slow bends by throwing me some fresh water from a bucket.'

2 July 1950. Grand Prix de l'ACF, Reims. F2
#34 José Froilán González. DNS
González was entered in 1600 with the unblown six-cylinder engine in the Formula 2 race at the Grand Prix de l'ACF in Reims but drove it only in practice. The same day Roberto 'Bitito' Mieres drove one of the ACA cars, the Ferrari 166 s/n 011F. For some reason the Maserati was not raced and González drove the Ferrari instead, but with no luck again as he had to stop with engine problems; Mieres could only watch from the pits. The race was won by Alberto Ascari with a Ferrari 166 F2. For the Formula 1 race González drove 4CLT 1599.

Exceptional Cars

1950: Fangio scores 1600's greatest victory

Grand Prix d'Albi 1950 – before the race Fangio, González and Bucci examine the supercharged engine re-installed in 1600 after two Formula 2 races. Unfortunately the supercharged engine failed in the race.
Ton Blankvoort collection

16 July 1950. Grand Prix d'Albi.
#10 Juan Manuel Fangio. DNF (engine)
Fangio was at the wheel of 1600 again for the Albi race in France. His friend Froilán González would drive the other Maserati. The competition was divided into two heats and a final. Fangio drove the first one, taking the lead from the beginning with Farina and Ascari behind him. On the fourth lap Ascari overtook Farina, while Fangio extended his lead. Then Farina was out and Ascari started to put pressure on Fangio, who in return set the lap record at 171km/h (106.2mph). After that, Ascari had to retire with engine problems and Sommer, aware of trouble with Fangio's car, started to cut the distance between them. With only two kilometres remaining, the Maserati began smoking with a damaged engine. Fangio managed to get to the chequered flag but only after Sommer's Talbot-Lago had overtaken him just a few metres before the finishing line.

For the final Fangio had no car to drive so González offered him his Maserati but *El Chueco* did not want his friend to lose the opportunity for victory. That did not happen as Froilán finished second overall behind Louis Rosier's Talbot-Lago.

23 July 1950. Grand Prix of Holland
#2 Juan Manuel Fangio. DNF (suspension)
A very disapppointing weekend for the Argentinians. González's Maserati 4CLT caught fire in the pits but he finally finished in seventh place, five laps behind the winner Louis Rosier with a Talbot-Lago T26C. Fangio, after battling for the lead with Rosier for 20 laps, had to retire with broken suspension.

12 November 1950. Gran Premio Ciudad de Paraná
#10 Onofre Marimón. 4th
After the European season the ACA drivers and cars returned to Argentina. In the city of Paraná in the province of Entre Ríos a few machines came together for a race. Fangio and González chose the two Ferrari 166FLs, long and short wheelbase respectively, so 4CLT 1600 was available for Onofre Marimón. It was obvious that the race was going to be won by Fangio or González if nothing strange happened, and that was the way it was. Alfredo Pian with a 4CLT took third place with Fangio's protegé, the rookie Marimón, fourth.

18 December 1950. Gran Premio del Presidente Alessandri. Santiago de Chile
#14 Louis Rosier. DNF
The first Grand Prix in Chile was organized with the help of the Automóvil Club Argentino. The ACA brought four cars, the two Ferrari 166s and the two Maserati 4CLTs, giving 1600 to Louis Rosier. The race was won by Fangio in a Ferrari, followed by González with the other 166, and in third place, two laps behind, came the Uruguayan Eitel Cantoni with his 4CLT. There was no luck for the French driver with the Maserati who had to retire on the sixth lap.

Maserati 4CLT | 57

1950: Fangio scores 1600's greatest victory

Postscript to 1600's international career

Maserati 4CLT 1600 was not used in 1951 but reappeared in March 1952 at the Autódromo de Buenos Aires driven by Carlos Menditeguy.

9 March 1952. Gran Premio del General Juan Perón y de la Ciudad de Buenos Aires. Autódromo de Buenos Aires
#44 Carlos Menditeguy. 6th

The inaugural race of the Autódromo de Buenos Aires was the Gran Premio del General Perón, a way for the Argentinian President to honour himself for building the new race track. It was primarily for local drivers but the Équipe Simca-Gordini used the competition to test its new cars. Once again, the race was won by Fangio, followed by González, both with the ACA Ferraris. Local sportsman and dandy 'Charlie' Menditeguy drove 1600 to sixth place, finishing two laps behind the leader.

- Fangio eases himself into 1600's cockpit for the last time. The 1950 Dutch Grand Prix was his final race in an ACA Maserati.
  Ton Blankvoort collection

- The front row of the grid at Zandvoort had Fangio in the centre, flanked by González and race winner Louis Rosier in a Talbot-Lago.
  Ton Blankvoort collection

Exceptional Cars

1950: Fangio scores 1600's greatest victory

In the Dutch Grand Prix, Fangio battled for the lead with Rosier but had to retire when 1600 suffered broken suspension.
Ton Blankvoort collection

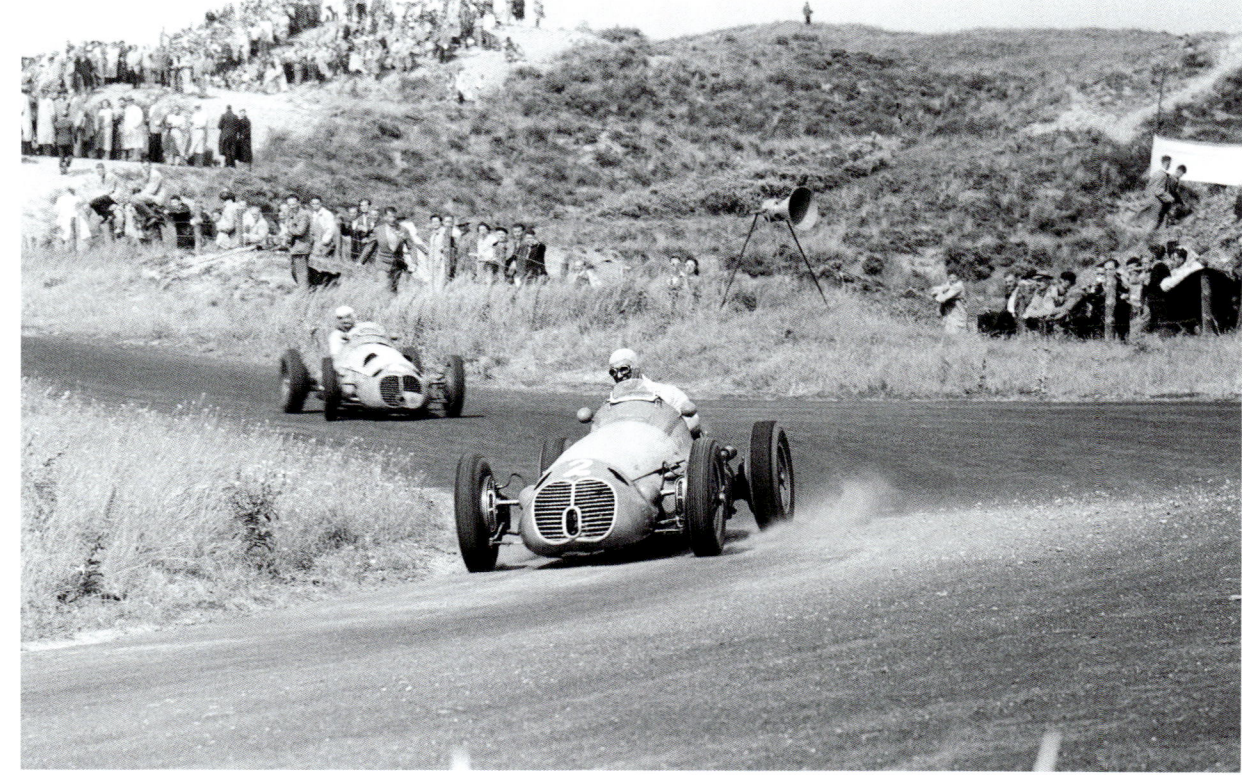

The two ACA Maseratis among the sand dunes at Zandvoort, racing in Europe for the last time. Note the bonnet air scoops on the González car (1599) and the enlarged radiator aperture on Fangio's leading 1600.
The Klemantaski Collection

Maserati 4CLT | 59

1950: Fangio scores 1600's greatest victory

16 March 1952. Gran Premio Extraordinario de Eva Duarte Perón. Autódromo de Buenos Aires
#44 Carlos Menditeguy. 2nd

The following week was the turn for the Evita Perón self-homage race at the same venue. The starting grid was similar, and the winner was Fangio, again with the LWB Ferrari 166FL, but in second place came Menditeguy with 1600. Fangio set the fastest time in qualifying followed by González with the SWB Ferrari 166FL. The race was Fangio's from the start with *El Cabezón* following him until he had to retire with problems in his Ferrari. Menditeguy took advantage of the situation and moved into second place where he stayed until the end of the race.

23 March 1952. Gran Premio de Uruguay. Piriápolis
#4 José Froilán González. DNF

Following the Argentinian events, a race was organized in Uruguay at the new circuit of Punta Fría in Piriápolis. The entry list was dominated by Argentinians and Brazilians with the addition of French drivers Maurice Trintignant, Louis Rosier, Robert Manzon and André Simon. The race was led from start to finish by Fangio with the LWB Ferrari 166FL followed by Chico Landi

● Drama in the pits at Zandvoort – González came in for a routine refuelling stop and tyre change but had to make a quick escape when spilt fuel caught fire and engulfed the car (1599). Amazingly, when it was extinguished, González was able to rejoin the race and came home in seventh place.
Ton Blankvoort collection

60 | Exceptional Cars

1950: Fangio scores 1600's greatest victory

with his Ferrari 375F1. Froilán González, in 4CLT 1600, managed only 19 laps of the 65-lap race.

**30 March 1952. Gran
Premio de Montevideo. Piriápolis**
#42 Carlos Fortunati Firpo. DNF
The following week there was a second race at the same track which was also won by Fangio followed by González with the other ACA Ferrari. Carlos Fortunati Firpo drove 1600 but failed to fInish.

**1 February 1953. Autódromo de la
Ciudad de Buenos Aires**
#42 Carlos Fortunati Firpo. DNF
After the Gran Premio de Argentina for Formula 1 cars at the Autódromo de Buenos Aires in January 1953, there was a race for Fórmula Libre called Gran Premio de la Ciudad de Buenos Aires. As the rules were open, the European teams used this race to test new ideas for the new season, but it was also a good opportunity to use old cars like the ACA Ferraris and Maseratis. On this occasion Carlos Fortunati Firpo drove 1600 but only lasted a few laps. The race was won by 'Nino' Farina with a Ferrari 500.

Carlos Menditeguy drove 1600 at the inaugural meeting of the Buenos Aires Autodrome in March 1952. He finished sixth in the first race and second in a follow-up event a week later.
whitefly.cc

Last recorded event for 1600 in its original form was 1953 Gran Premio de Argentina at the Buenos Aires Autodrome where it was driven by Carlos Fortunati Firpo. It failed to finish.
whitefly.cc

Maserati 4CLT

José Froilán González
The British called him the Pampas Bull

A highlight in the career of *El Cabezón* was winning the 1954 Le Mans 24 Hours with Maurice Trintignant (right in picture) *LAT Images*

González, 'Pepe' to his friends, Froilán for most people, and in many cases *El Cabezón* (Fat Head), or *The Pampas Bull* in the British press, was one of the most popular Argentinian racing drivers of the post-war era. He was born in Arrecifes, a city in the north of the province of Buenos Aires in 1922 as the first-born of the family which would later include a sister, María Victoria, and a brother, Oscar León.

He was very good at all sports, not only race driving, but more than that, he was very competitive. His father had a Chevrolet dealership so he was surrounded by cars from childhood. One of his friends, Rafael Sierra, head of the Automóvil Club Argentino for many years, told the author a story that depicts Pepe's personality during his early days. One day, a client arrived at the showroom with a Jaguar SS that he wanted to sell. He left the car and 'Pepe' looked for his friend to go for a ride. They took the car and, without permission, drove from Arrecifes to Salto and back, covering more than 60 kilometres.

His début in motor racing was in 1946 driving a Fuerza Limitada single-seater. A few months after that, on a trip to Buenos Aires, he saw a Dodge in a dealership and was instantly tempted. He managed to gather the money and bought it and soon after entered the 1947 Mil Millas Argentinas for stock cars with Bernardo Pérez as co-driver. Luck was not on their side as they suffered from various mechanical problems until, finally, the engine blew up.

Pepe's next race was the 1948 Gran Premio de América del Sur, driving a Chevrolet that Pérez had prepared in Arrecifes. They were able to hold fourth place for a while but the race was so tough that they had many problems and once again retired. In the Mil Millas of the same year, again with Pérez, they were doing very well until they had an accident that badly damaged the car.

In Mecánica Nacional Fuerza Libre he raced with success during 1948 and 1949 with a Ford V8 christened '9 de Julio', achieving 11 victories. This was the begining of a profesional career as González was then one of a small group of drivers that would travel to Europe to compete in the international races for single-seaters.

In Europe he was part of the ACA team that included his friend and rival Juan Manuel Fangio, Clemar Bucci, Benedicto Campos and Onofre Marimón amongst others. He was very active driving Maserati 4CLs and 4CLTs (including 1600) and also the two Ferrari 166FLs that the team had bought in 1949.

1950: Fangio scores 1600's greatest victory

After good showings in a series of non-championship races in 1950 and a fantastic win at the V Gran Premio del General Juan Perón y de la Ciudad de Buenos Aires in January 1951 driving a Ferrari 166FL against a trio of Mercedes-Benz W154s, he landed a seat in one of the Scuderia Ferrari cars for selected races.

His début in World Championship races was in Bremgarten, Switzerland driving a Talbot-Lago T26C without success. The relationship with Scuderia Ferrari started with a terrific second place in France, sharing a 375 with Alberto Ascari. The first of his two wins in Formula 1 came at the following race at Silverstone when he defeated his friend and rival Fangio and all the Alfettas, a feat that gained great respect from *Commendatore* Enzo Ferrari as it was the first win for his team in a World Championship Formula 1 race.

González raced in 26 Grands Prix over nine seasons, winning on two occasions, both at Silverstone. He took three pole positions, set six fastest laps and his best placing in the World Championship was second, in 1954.

Making his name – González at the wheel of his Mecánica Nacional Fuerza Libre Ford V8 in 1949. *Revista Froilán*

González, right of picture with Fangio, as Charles Faroux, veteran journalist and Clerk of the Course at the Monaco Grand Prix, talks to Maserati mechanic Amadeo Bignami. *Museo Fangio*

Maserati 4CLT | 63

1950: Fangio scores 1600's greatest victory

He never felt comfortable in open-road racing, which is why he rarely drove stock cars and was never attracted by the Mille Miglia, but one of his career highlights was victory in the 1954 24 Hours of Le Mans driving a Ferrari 375 Plus with Maurice Trintignant.

When he withdrew from the international scene, he was very successful in Mecánica Nacional Fuerza Libre driving a Ferrari single-seater with Chevrolet Corvette engine and winning the championship in 1958 and 1959. After retiring as a driver, he stayed involved in racing as the manager of a Mecánica Nacional team and also with stock cars and prototypes.

'Pepe' was always very friendly with people coming to his Fiat dealership in Buenos Aires, happy to talk about racing until his very last days.

'I was apolitical, but always a Perónist. Once Perón asked me if we needed anything so we told him - a circuit! And then Perón built the Autódromo de Buenos Aires.

'Back then, almost every driver was fat, including Juan (Fangio) and me. When we were racing in Europe with the ACA team, we stayed in Galliate, so we used to go on bicycles to Novara which was about 20km away. But from time to time I stopped for a *prosciutto* sandwich on the way and waited for the boys to come back to rejoin them…'

José Froilán González died on 15 June 2013. He was 90 years old.

- González and Trintignant in the 4.9-litre Ferrari 375 Plus had a race-long duel with the Jaguars in the wet 1954 Le Mans 24 Hours. It was his best result in sports car racing. *LAT Images*

- The day of reckoning – González in the 4.5-litre Ferrari wins the 1951 British Grand Prix at Silverstone ahead of Fangio in his 1.5-litre Alfa Romeo 159. It marked the end of the domination by the supercharged Alfetta in Formula 1. *LAT Images*

Exceptional Cars

Onofre Agustín Marimón
Fangio's protegé who promised so much

● Onofre Marimón drove 1600 just once at the start of his international career. He died in 1954 before realizing his full potential. *LAT Images*

Onofre Marimón. Known as *Pinocho*, he was born in Zárate, in the province of Buenos Aires, the son of a very popular stock car driver, Domingo 'Toscanito' Marimón – who was given the nickname as he always had a Tuscan cigar in his mouth. His death at the age of 30 was a great shock for the whole racing scene, especially the Argentinian drivers.

Marimón made his racing début in 1949, winning a race in the coastal city of Mar del Plata driving his father's Chevrolet. During that year he finished second behind José Froilán González at a Mecánica Nacional race in La Cumbre, Córdoba, driving a car named *La Petisa* that was prepared by Toto Fangio, Juan Manuel's younger brother. He was very successful in single-seaters during the two years that he raced in Argentina before going to Europe, achieving a third place in the Fuerza Libre championship in 1950 behind Héctor Niemiz and Benedicto Campos.

In November 1950 Marimón had his one and only drive in Maserati 4CLT 1600 at the Gran Premio Ciudad de Paraná in which he finished fourth. The following year he travelled to Europe under Fangio's guidance, having his first outing at Le Mans sharing a Talbot-Lago T26GS with José Froilán González but failed to finish the race. Later that year he drove a Maserati 4CLT from the Scuderia Milano in the French Grand Prix at Reims but again had to abandon because of engine failure.

During 1952 he raced in Argentina and returned to Europe to drive with Juan Manuel Fangio at the 24 Hours of Le Mans with the Alfa Romeo 3000CM – another retirement. In 1953 he raced on five occasions for the Maserati team, driving the A6GCM. Third place in his début at Spa-Francorchamps was his best result.

The 1954 Formula 1 season saw Marimón driving for Maserati again. At the British Grand Prix at Silverstone he was on the podium after an amazing jump from 28th on the starting grid to third place at the end of the race.

The 1954 German Grand Prix at the Nürburgring would be the first European Formula 1 event to have a fatality. Early in the morning practice, Marimón lost control of his Maserati 250F going through a third gear turn. Juan Manuel Fangio was following him in the Mercedes-Benz. *Pinocho* would die on the way to hospital. Inspection of the car by Fangio and González found that the gear lever was in fourth. For the Argentinians the European racing scene would never be quite the same again.

1950: Fangio scores 1600's greatest victory

Louis Rosier
A Frenchman in the Argentine team

Louis Rosier was born in Chapdes-Beaufort in central France in 1905. His début in racing was in 1924 riding a 1,000cc motor cycle. Some years later, due to his friendship with Yves Giraud-Cabantous and Philippe Etancelin, he had his first race in a car, a blown 1.1-litre SCAP which he used for hill-climbs.

During World War II, Rosier served in the Résistance, and later was able to travel across Europe to free his wife and daughter from a concentration camp. When the war was over, he returned to racing at the Grand Prix du Roussillon at Perpignan where he finished sixth in a Talbot-Lago.

His name and Talbot were to write history together. In 1947 he won the Grand Prix at Albi and in 1948 and 1949 the Coupe du Salon at Montlhéry. He created his own team called Écurie Rosier for himself and guest drivers first with Talbot-Lago T26Cs and then racing a Maserati 250F and Ferrari 500.

In 1950 he reached the zenith of his career when winning the Le Mans 24 Hours in a Talbot-Lago T26GS with his son Jean-Louis - who drove for just two laps. His début in Formula 1 was at the British Grand Prix in 1950 with a Talbot-Lago with which he finished in fifth position behind the three Alfa Romeos and his team-mate Yves Giraud-Cabantous. At the end of the year he was invited by the ACA to drive 1600 in the inaugural race in Chile.

Back in Europe with the Talbot in 1951, he scored only a fourth place in the Belgian Grand Prix. Talbot-Lago decided to quit racing for the following season so Rosier decided to buy a Ferrari 500 to compete in Formula 2, with which he finished second at Pau and won at Albi and Cadours. He scored no points in the World Championships in the following years until his last race at the Nürburgring in 1956 where he placed fifth.

On 29 October 1956, Rosier flipped his Ferrari 750 Monza at the beginning of the Coupe du Salon which had started in heavy rain. He was trapped and suffered head injuries and died three weeks later at the Neuilly-sur-Seine hospital. He was 51 years old.

● A tough Frenchman who would go on to win Le Mans almost single-handed, Rosier drove 1600 only once, in a guest appearance for the ACA team in Santiago, Chile. *LAT Images*

Carlos Mediteguy
All-round sportsman who reached Formula 1

Carlos Mediteguy was not only a racing driver but a true sportsman. He was one of those public figures that do not exist anymore: a charming man, a great dancer, polo player and golfer – and Formula 1 driver.

His début in motor racing was with a victory at the wheel of a Ferrari 166MM Touring Barchetta. For the Argentine Temporada in 1950 the Automóvil Club Argentino organized a sports car race in Mar del Plata on the Atlantic coast. The ACA lent one of the cars to Mediteguy who finished in front of another stylish driver, Roberto 'Bitito' Mieres with his Alfa Romeo 8C 2300 Monza.

'Charlie' first participated in the Turismo de Carretera in the Vuelta de Coronel Pringles in 1952 and finished in 13th place. Victory with stock cars came late in his career, at Olvarría in 1956.

One of the most popular stories in local motor racing is from when he was leading a race and, only a few kilometres from the finish, the engine broke. He got out of the car, gave a cigarette lighter to his co-driver and said: '*Quémelo Linares, quémelo*' ('Burn it Linares, burn it').

Also in 1952, he drove Maserati 4CLT 1600 in two Fórmula Libre races of the early-season Argentine Temporada, finishing second in Gran Premio de Eva Duarte Perón to Juan Manuel Fangio in the ACA Ferrari 166FL.

Back in sports cars, he shared a Maserati 300S with Stirling Moss for the 1000 Kilómetros de la Ciudad de Buenos Aires in January 1956. He got used to the car very quickly and set a pace very similar to his team-mate. They finished two laps ahead of Oliver Gendebien and Phil Hill with a Ferrari 860 Monza.

He did not finish on his Formula 1 début with a Gordini at the 1953 Argentine Grand Prix. The following year he started the local Grand Prix with a Maserati A6GCM but suffered engine problems. From 1955 to 1958 he raced on nine occasions with the Maserati team at the wheel of a 250F, with third place in the 1957 Argentine GP his best result. His last race in Formula 1 was with a Cooper T51 at the Argentine GP in 1960, where he finished in fourth.

Carlos Mediteguy retired from racing in 1967 and a year later he participated in the film *Turismo de Carretera*. He died in Buenos Aires in 1973 at the age of 57.

- Carlos Mediteguy starred in all sports before and after becoming a racing driver. Two races in 1600 came early in his career, the greatest achievement of which was winning the Buenos Aires 1000Km with Stirling Moss. *whitefly.cc*

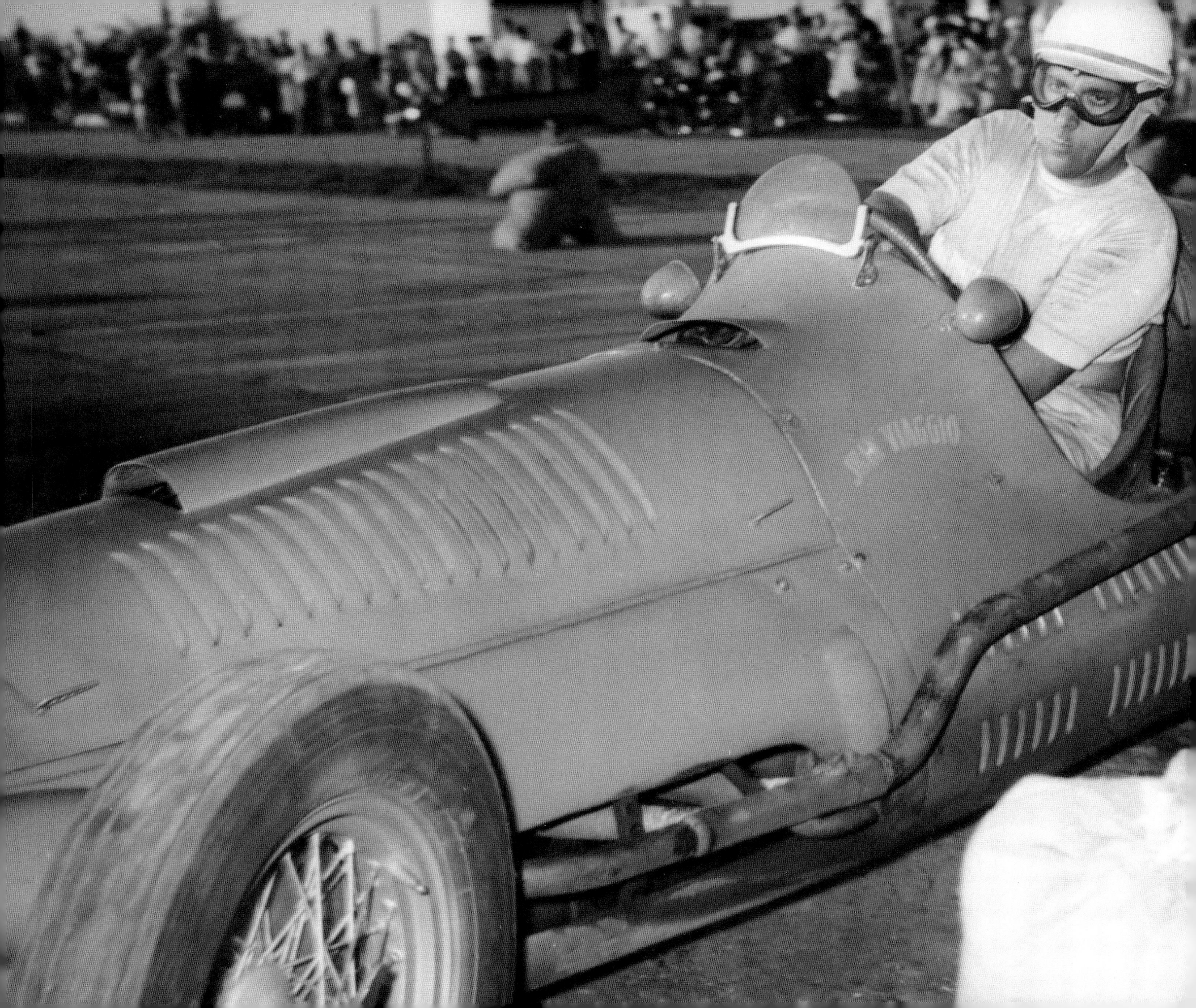

Part 3
Transplant: 1600 with a Ford V8

The 4CLT 1600 was retired from racing after the Gran Premio de la Ciudad de Buenos Aires on 1 February 1953. After that, it sat in one of the ACA warehouses along with other racing cars and spares that included not only pieces for the two 4CLTs and the two 166s but also a lot for pre-war Alfa Romeos.

For the 1955 season the rules changed for the Mecánica Nacional Fuerza Libre class. Instead of allowing only locally-produced engines and chassis, it was opened to international Grand Prix cars more than five years old, still with locally-built engines.

That was an opportunity for the ACA to make some money. So the two 4CLTs were sold, 1599 to Luis Brosutti, who fitted it with a Studebaker V8, and 1600 to Juan Viaggio, an amateur driver whose day job was that of a surgeon.

With the technical help of Eng. 'Pancho' Lucius, Viaggio's Maserati was fitted with a Ford V8 engine. His first mechanic was called Farina, but after a few races the car was prepared by Omar Fillo, who did it as a hobby and was, according to 'Coca', Viaggio's widow, 'a romantic who didn't mind staying up all night working on the car'.

When Viaggio first ran the Maserati, it was still painted in the Argentine racing colours of blue with a yellow bonnet but for some unknown reason he decided to paint it red.

Viaggio raced 1600 for only two years. During that period he finished in all but one of the 11 races entered. His best placing was third.

● New life for an old car – amateur driver Juan Viaggio adapted 4CLT 1600 for Mecánica Nacional Fuerza Libre by fitting a Ford V8 and raced it for two seasons, 1955 and 1956. *whitefly.cc*

Chapter 5
Rebirth for Mecánica Nacional Fuerza Libre

In the 1940s and 1950s, the rules for motor racing in Argentina were very lax. They had to be because of the scarcity of suitable cars. Many came to race when they were old or obsolete in Europe and the US. They ran in a class called Fuerza Libre, which meant more-or-less no restrictions. For those built or modified locally, the races were Mecánica Nacional Fuerza Libre, while the cars built outside Argentina, sometimes Grand Prix or sports-racing cars, were just called Specials.

The variety of cars made these series very colourful. They included big, aero-engined machines like the 8.2-litre Chandler-Curtiss and small supercharged vintage Bugattis. Some of the imports stayed untouched but the fate for most was that of most racing cars – modification, looking for more performance.

The free formula series became more and more popular after amateur drivers, inspired by watching the international races, were tempted to build their own specials to take part either in Fuerza Limitada, the small class, or Fuerza Libre races. Both were loosely governed by the Mecánica Nacional regulations.

Maserati 4CLT 1600 started racing as a Grand Prix car but was modified to fit the Mecánica Nacional Fuerza Libre with the adoption of a locally-built Ford engine.

For Mecánica Nacional Fuerza Libre, the rules were just a guide, because the aim was to have as many contenders as possible, and from many different parts of the country, just as in stock car racing. So, basically, they said that the car had to have a locally-built engine and full bodywork. There was no limit to engine capacity, supercharging was permitted, and there was no mention of weight. It was very simple: after all, Libre means 'free'.

Installing the Ford V8

An article by journalist Juan C. Valente published in the Argentinian magazine *Coche a la Vista* in September 1956 described the work done by Dr. Juan Viaggio to Maserati 4CLT 1600 to fit the Mecánica Nacional Fuerza Libre rules. What follows is a loose translation of Mr Valente's article.

Doctor Juan A Viaggio, an avid motor sport enthusiast, had a problem. In his eagerness to progress in racing he wanted replace his car and another he co-owned with one of his associates with one which would be suitable for motor sport events throughout Argentina. Eminently practical as well as a very busy man, he sought to avoid the frustrations of building a car from scratch and, knowing of a change to the Fuerza Libre regulations, he opted to buy the chassis and body of a Grand Prix car, in which he would instal a locally-built engine.

He agreed to buy one of the Maserati 4CLTs from the Automóvil Club Argentino that had been raced in Europe in the early post-war period. This car was identical to that acquired, for the same reasons, by Luis E Brosutti.

The chassis was kept as built by Maserati, with the minimum of modifications to allow the installation of

Installing the Ford V8 required some modifications to the tubular chassis but the basics of the car remained unchanged. Among the evolving bodywork alterations was an air scoop on the engine cover to feed the three carburettors atop the engine. *whitefly.cc*

70 | Exceptional Cars

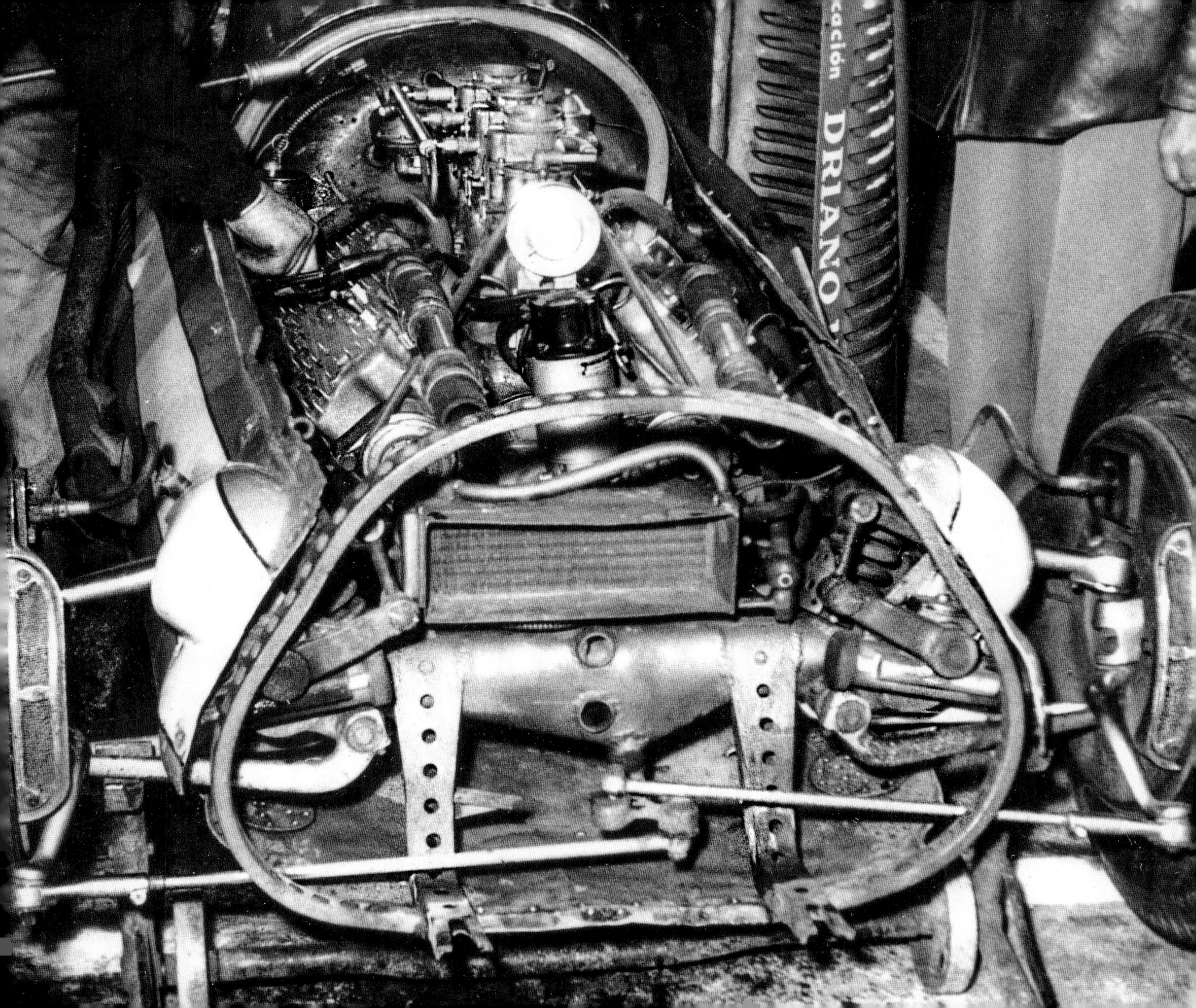
cación
DRIANO

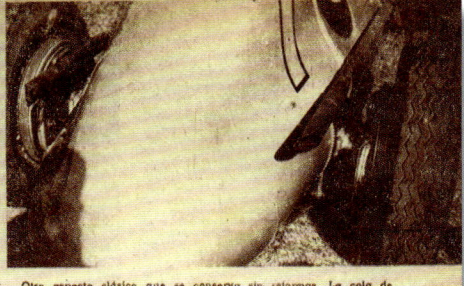

- Technical details of Mecánica Nacional cars from the 1950s are scarce. The author is indebted to this article from *Coche a la Vista* for the material in this chapter.

Rebirth for Mecánica Nacional Fuerza Libre

The surgeon who made the transplant. Juan Viaggio commissioned the Maserati-Ford, drove it for two years and after he retired from motor racing, enjoyed success in power boat racing. *whitefly.cc*

the new engine. Viaggio chose a 4.6-litre Ford V8 of the kind that powered Ford production models and which, in standard form, was rated at 100hp.

The installation was the work of a group of engineers, particularly Francisco Lucius and Omar Fillol, at the workshops of Fillol and Berardi in San Isidro.

The engine dimensions are 84.1mm bore and 101.6mm stroke, giving a total displacement of 4,600cc. The pistons are in aluminium alloy and the connecting rods and crankshaft are standard Ford. The compression ratio is 9.5:1. Lubrication is by an Edelbrock dry sump system using two Ford oil pumps.

The single camshaft, from Rabbah or Vignoleti, is gear-driven from the crankshaft and operates the valves with pushrods. The inlet valves are 41mm diameter, the exhaust 38mm. Double valve springs and Edelbrock 'headers' (manifolds) were added.

A team of three 35mm twin-choke carburettors are fed by a Ford fuel pump from the standard Maserati 190-litre tank. The ignition system uses a Scintilla magneto, a Lincoln distributor, and Champion H9 spark plugs.

The engine's power was increased from the standard unit [frustratingly, Mr Valente does not tell us by how much] to reach high speeds, as this superb chassis provides optimum service in all sorts of race conditions. The dry weight of Dr Viaggio's car is 750kg.

Extracts from the Argentine Motor Sport Regulations 1953

Article 73
The car race events taking place in the Republic of Argentina will be divided into five categories, each having the right to a respective championship:

a) Coches Especiales (Specials)
b) Coches Mecánica Nacional Fuerza Libre
c) Coches Mecánica Nacional Fuerza Limitada
d) Coches Sport (Sports cars)
e) Coches Turismo de Carretera (Stock cars)

Organisers, with prior agreement from the CDA (the controlling body), will be allowed to stage events for cars that do not fall into these categories. These events will not qualify for championship points.

In exceptional circumstances, and with authorization after prior consideration of each particular case, cars of different categories that do not strictly comply with Articles 74, 75, 76, 77 and 78 may be admitted.

Article 74
Coches Especiales
Included in this category are all racing cars (including Grand Prix) of any provenance and cylinder capacity, with or without supercharging. Organisers can, with prior agreement from the CDA, admit in this category other cars prepared to equivalent standards.

Article 75
Coches Mecánica Nacional Fuerza Libre
Engine: Produced in large series for touring cars, or entirely built in this country, with drawings to be presented to the CDA for approval.

Capacity/displacement: Free.

Supercharging: Permitted.

Chassis: Built entirely in this country, or from original touring car, modified in this country [This clause was modified from 1955 to allow the use of imported racing car chassis more than five years old].

Bodywork: Special racing bodywork must be complete and without temporary elements. The same applies to the engine cover, nose and tail, which must present a smooth line.

Maserati 4CLT | 73

Chapter 6
Racing career with Juan Viaggio

6 March 1955. Gran Premio Autódromo de la Ciudad de Buenos Aires
#7 Juan Viaggio. 4th
Dr. Juan Viaggio made his début with the Maserati-Ford at the beginning of the 1955 season. It was the first of two races at the Autódromo de Buenos Aires for the series under the new regulations. He finished in fourth place - not bad for an amateur.

14 March 1955. II Gran Premio Autódromo Municipal
 # 7 Juan Viaggio. 4th
During the weekend there was a series of races for bicycles, sports cars and Mecánica Nacional single-seaters. *Velocidad* magazine wrote that Jorge Daponte with a Chevrolet had great opposition from Juan Viaggio fighting for third place, but finally he overtook him, leaving the Maserati fourth. The race was won by José Féliz López with a Chevrolet.

March 1955. II Carrera del Recuerdo Vicente López
#7 Juan Viaggio. 3rd
The second edition of this race had fewer cars on the grid for various reasons. It was held on the Ruta Panamericana which made it a competition half-way between a street and a circuit race. Jesús Ricardo Iglesias was one of the favourite drivers to win but had to retire when the engine of his car exploded. Alfredo Pian then assumed the lead and took a well deserved victory in his Ford, followed by Gilberto Riega in a Volpi-Wayne and completing the podium was Juan Viaggio, six laps behind the winner.

April 1955. Rosario
#7 Juan Viaggio. 5th
The Circuito Parque Independencia was one of the many parks used for racing before the construction of the purpose-built racing circuits. It still exists as a park but is no longer used for racing. The final 25-lap race was won by Alfredo Pian with his Ford V8-engined special, followed Requejo and Daponde. In fifth place came Viaggio with the Maserati-Ford, one lap behind the winner.

July 1955. Premio Independencia. Autódromo 17 de Octubre, Buenos Aires
#7 Juan Viaggio. 14th
The winter race at the Autódromo de Buenos Aires was dominated by Alfredo Pián with his Ford. It was not a good event for Viaggio who covered only 14 of the 20 laps.

October 1955. Premio General Belgrano. Autódromo 17 de Octubre, Buenos Aires
#7 Juan Viaggio. 6th
A much better result than the previous race at the Autódromo for Viaggio who finished sixth, just one lap behind the winner Jesús Ricardo Iglesias.

October 1955. San Nicolás
#7 Juan Viaggio. DNF
This competition was held on a dirt track in San Nicolás in the province of Buenos Aires. Viaggio failed to finish, for reasons unknown.

Dr. Juan Viaggio is seen leaving the pits of the Autódromo de Buenos Aires during the first season with the Ford-powered Maserati in July 1955. *whitefly.cc*

Exceptional Cars

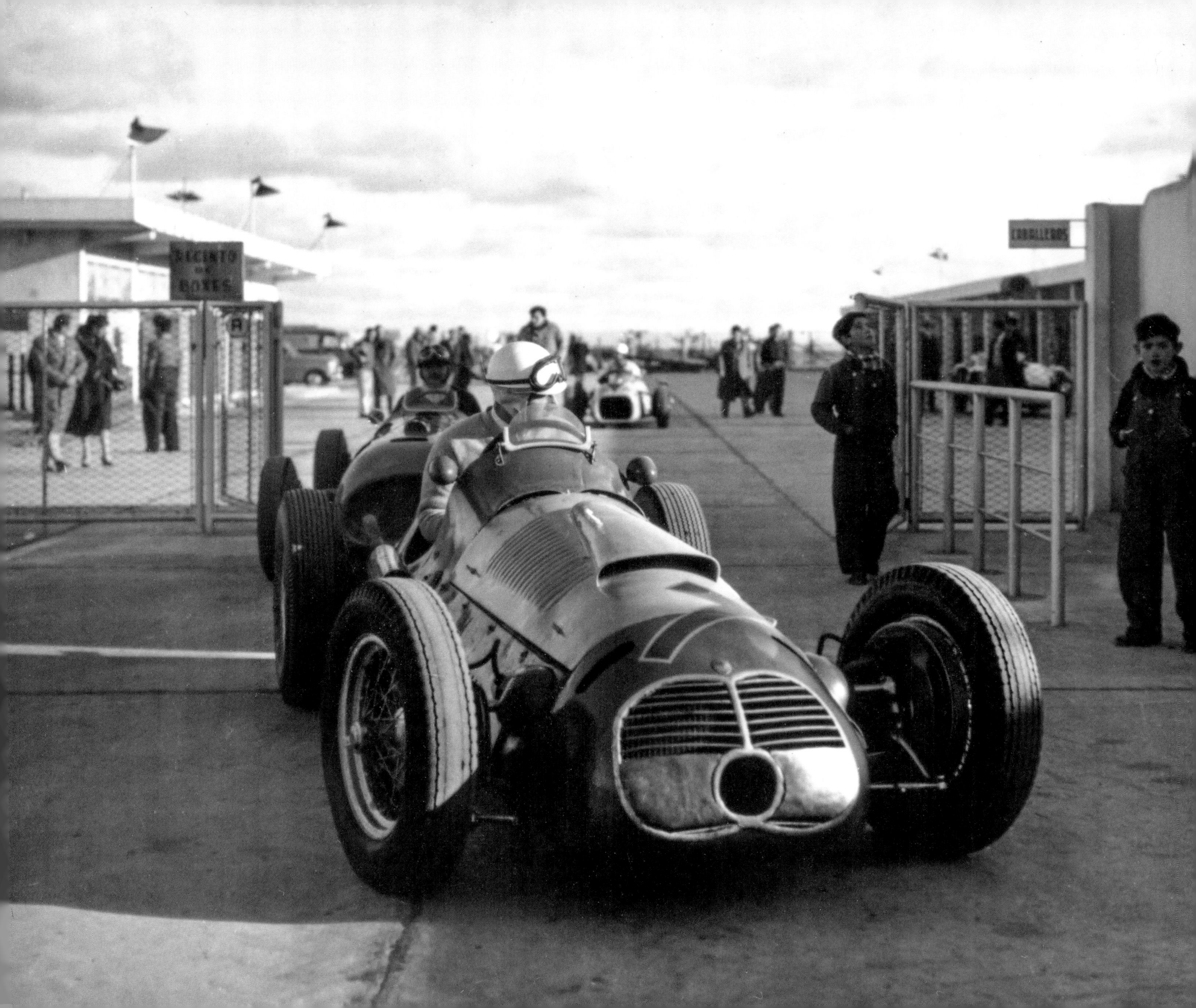
RECINTO
BOXES
CABALLEROS

Racing career with Juan Viaggio

17 June 1956. 500 Millas Argentinas, Rafaela
#7 Juan Viaggio. 6th
The 1956 edition of the famous Rafaela 500 brought a weird mix of cars. The organizers made two races into one, having sports cars and Mecánica Nacional single-seaters share the same grid but starting the slower sports cars first and the *monoposti* 30 seconds later. The overall result shows just how eclectic the race was. It was won by Carlos Najurieta with his Ferrari 375MM Pinin Farina Spyder with a total time of 4h 45m 59s followed by Jesús Ricardo Iglesias with his Chevrolet-Wayne, then Ricardo Grandío with a Maserati A6GCS, Alfredo Pian's Ford, Luis Milán with a Ferrari 625TF and Juan Viaggio in sixth place in the Maserati-Ford. He was pictured in *Velocidad* magazine at a pit stop, refuelling and changing spark plugs.

July 1956. Parque Independencia, Rosario
Juan Viaggio. 8th
No information on this race could be found, other than the result for Viaggio.

- In March 1955 Viaggio achieved his best result with the Maserati, finishing third in the Carrera del Recuerdo on a road circuit in Vicente López, Buenos Aires.
  whitefly.cc

- Missing its nose cone and the oil tank cap, Viaggio passes the grandstands at the Autódromo de Buenos Aires in March 1955.
  whitefly.cc

Exceptional Cars

Racing career with Juan Viaggio

October 1956. Premio Río de la Plata.
Costanera Sur, Buenos Aires
#7 Juan Viaggio. 4th

The Buenos Aires Moto Club organized a street race at the Costanera Sur in Buenos Aires near the Río de la Plata. There were two competitions, for Mecánica Nacional Fuerza Limitada and Fuerza Libre. The bigger-engined class was won by Alfredo Pian with a Ford V8-powered car and Viaggio with the Maserati-Ford finished in fourth place, two minutes behind the leader.

14 October 1956. El Pinar, Uruguay
#7 Juan Viaggio. 5th

Like Argentina, Uruguay has always had a great deal of enthusiasm for motor racing, especially for home-made specials like the Mecánica Nacional single-seaters which owed more to personal effort than engineering. This was the case for the El Pinar race that was won by the Uruguayan Asdrúbal Fontes Bayardo defeating the very competitive Argentinians. Behind him were José Félix López and Ramón Requejo, in fourth place Miguel

As with most Mecánica Nacional cars, the Maserati-Ford evolved race-by-race. Here it is showing a modified nose section, probably at Rosario. *whitefly.cc*

Maserati 4CLT | 77

Racing career with Juan Viaggio

The Maserati-Ford in its last configuration at the Parque Independencia in Rosario in July 1956. *whitefly.cc*

Luzzardo with a Maserati chassis using a Lincoln engine, and in fifth place Dr. Viaggio with his Maserati-Ford.

19 May 1957. San Nicolás
Juan Viaggio / José Félix Lopes. DNS

The story behind this mysterious race starts with a note on a picture that says: 'San Nicolás 19/05/1957'. It shows three cars, none of which look like Viaggio's. On the other side, there were notes and comments stating that José Félix Lopes had driven Viaggio's car on one occasion and that he had lost his life in it. We asked 'Coca' Viaggio, Juan's widow, about this. She mentioned that her husband had sold the car to José Félix Lopes but he did not get to race it as he died in a crash in practice for what was to be its first outing.

This episode is still not clear. For some reason, Lópes was driving his old car rather than the newly-acquired Maserati in practice when he lost control and crashed. 'Coca' remembers it as a big drama as Lopes' wife was at the circuit with one or two children. After the accident Viaggio, who was there just as a spectator, took care of the family and took them back to Buenos Aires in his car.

After this event, Juan Viaggio told his wife that he was not going to race again but he did in fact make a comeback with his old Gordini-Ford. His last races were in the Torneo Triangular in 1960. Maserati 4CLT 1600 was not seen again until it turned up with Lucio Bollaert in the late 1970s.

Racing career with Juan Viaggio

Juan Viaggio worked as a surgeon during the week and enjoyed motor racing at the weekends. He finished in eighth position at Rosario (top right) and had his last race in the Maserati in October 1956 at Río de la Plata. He had no race wins but took the chequered flag to finish at all but one of the events he entered.
whitefly.cc

Maserati 4CLT | 79

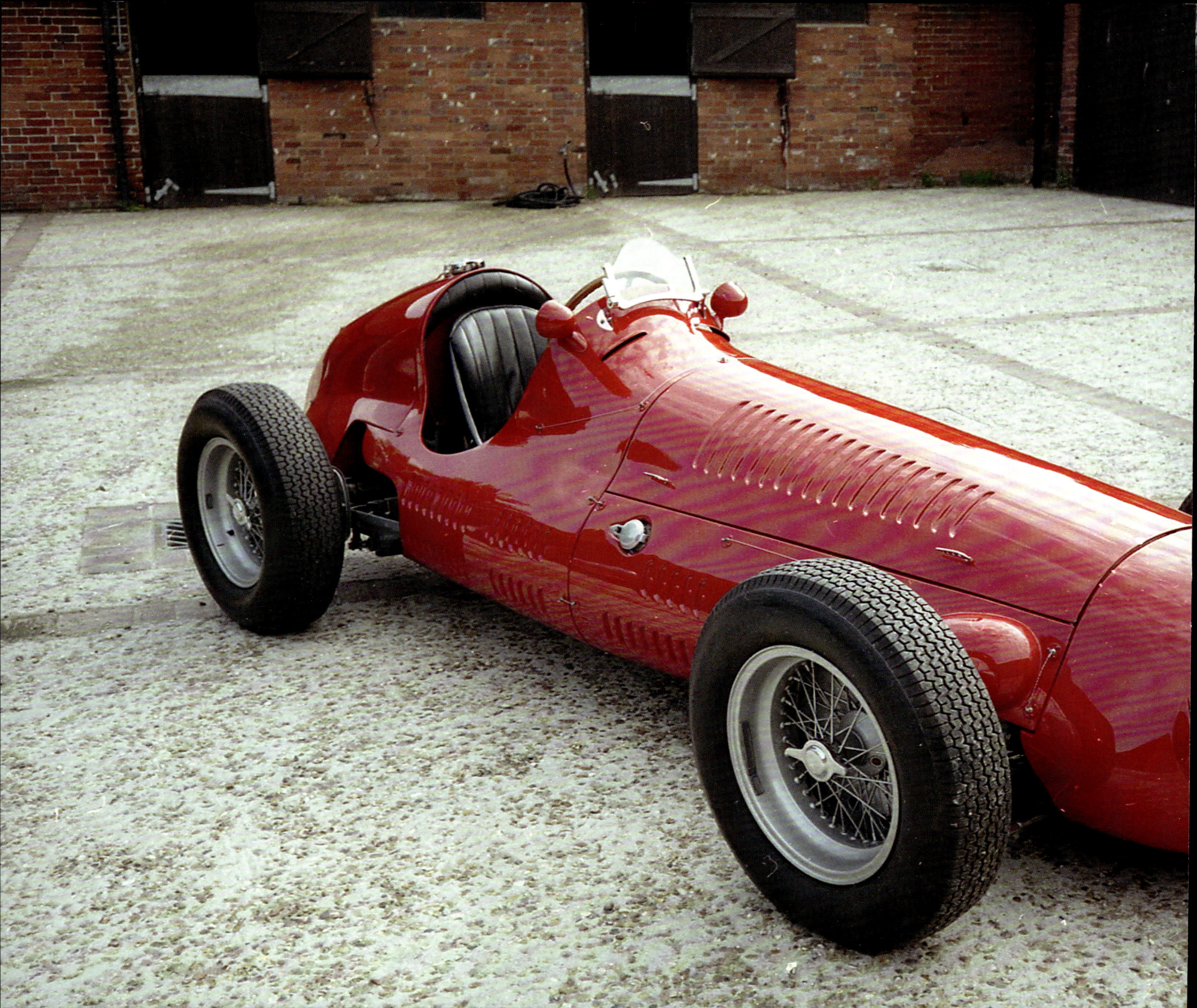

Part 4
Found and restored

4CLT 1600 after its long voyage – literally and metaphorically – from Argentina. It was restored to original specification in the United States, sold to Japan, and pictured here at Tony Merrick's premises after it had arrived in England in 1996.
Tony Merrick

The fate of the sports cars that re-appeared in Argentina in the 1970s and 1980s is pretty much known. For single-seaters the situation is much more complex.

To begin with, the rules for the Mecánica Nacional series allowed the use of obsolete chassis frames from established race car manufacturers but not the engines, so some cars came into Argentina incomplete or were simply separated from their engine and transmission. In the case of the two Maserati 4CLTs that the ACA had in storage after their international racing career came to an end, both were sold in 1955 without the engines, which were of no use to their new owners.

These cars were used and abused in different types of races: on street circuits, park tracks, and even dirt ovals such as Rafaela. They evolved race by race, both mechanically and aerodynamically, so after a few seasons they looked pretty much like something else. To trace the history of the two 4CLTs that raced in Fuerza Libre is not an easy task but thanks to the research done by architect Guillermo Sánchez, we know how 1599 evolved in shape so were are able to distinguish that car from 1600.

That was the starting point for unravelling 4CLT 1600's fate after it stopped racing. It is a fascinating journey, from South to North America, Japan, and eventually back to Europe, where it was fully restored to its specification in 1950, the time of the car's greatest achievements.

Chapter 7
Mystery in Argentina

In the old days when a Maserati, a Ferrari, or a Bugatti was an obsolete car in need of parts, there were just a few names buying, restoring, driving and trading them: 'Bubby' Salzman, Lucio Bollaert, Ernesto Dillon and Héctor Mendizábal were among the most active.

It is not exactly known who found 1600 and where it was. What we now know is that the car was not owned by Guillermo Vago, as stated in *Trident*, the magazine of the UK Maserati Club, in 1978. In a telephone conversation with 'Coto' Girelli in August 2018 he confirmed to this author that Vago had bought a Maserati single-seater from Uruguay and acquired many Maserati parts from different sources to restore the car. It seems most likely that this car was the ex-Fontes Bayardo 4CLT serial no.1608, as Fontes Bayardo was Uruguayan.

The first proof of the re-appearance of 1600 was found in Héctor Mendizábal's archive. Working on the book *Ferrari Argentina – Sports Cars* with Dr. Estanislao Iacona, we visited Mendizábal looking for pictures, stories and documents for the project. This was around 2005 and sadly, 'Pochi' Mendizábal was very ill, though still very interested in sharing his passion for cars, antiques and art. A few months after our last visit to his house he passed away. We had some photographs and negatives that he had given us to scan so we decided to return them to the two people that had been working with him in an office in the cellar of his house. That day we asked if there were more pictures of other cars and the answer was: 'Of course'. We opened a box and there was all kinds of stuff, including two sets of pictures of a Maserati 4CLT.

One of the sets was five black-and-white shots of a car in the garage of a house. At first, and because of the similarity to a set of pictures of the Maserati 8CL s/n 3034, we thought it could be Puopolo's 4CLT, but once we scanned them and enlarged the dashboard image, the number 1600 could be seen clearly on the identification plate.

The car was more-or-less complete with its engine, gearbox, and suspension. Only the body panels were missing. The other photo set was in colour and showed at least three different situations. There was no doubt that these pictures were of the same car, although there were some differences like the radiator.

One image shows the car in front of a house and near a bearing shop called Rulemanes Oscar. There are three people: a mechanic, someone with his back to the camera and… Lucio Bollaert.

We met Lucio Bollaert in 2001, again with Lao Iacona, and with Simon Moore when he was working on the new edition of his book *The Immortal 2.9*. We went to Bollaert's house in Pilar, about an hour north of Buenos Aires but unfortunately he was suffering a mental illness that prevented him from sharing any memories. We saw a room full of spares and other materials but nothing related to a 4CLT. So the only link between Lucio Bollaert and 4CLT 1600 was this single picture.

While writing these lines I received a reply to one of my queries from Alejandro García del Bo, a Club Alfa Romeo Argentina member, confirming that the shop Rulemanes Oscar was in Pilar with the exact

● After more than 30 years, destiny put the Maserati back on an ACA trailer. This is probably the first photo of 1600 after it came to light in the early 1980s. *whitefly.cc*

82 | Exceptional Cars

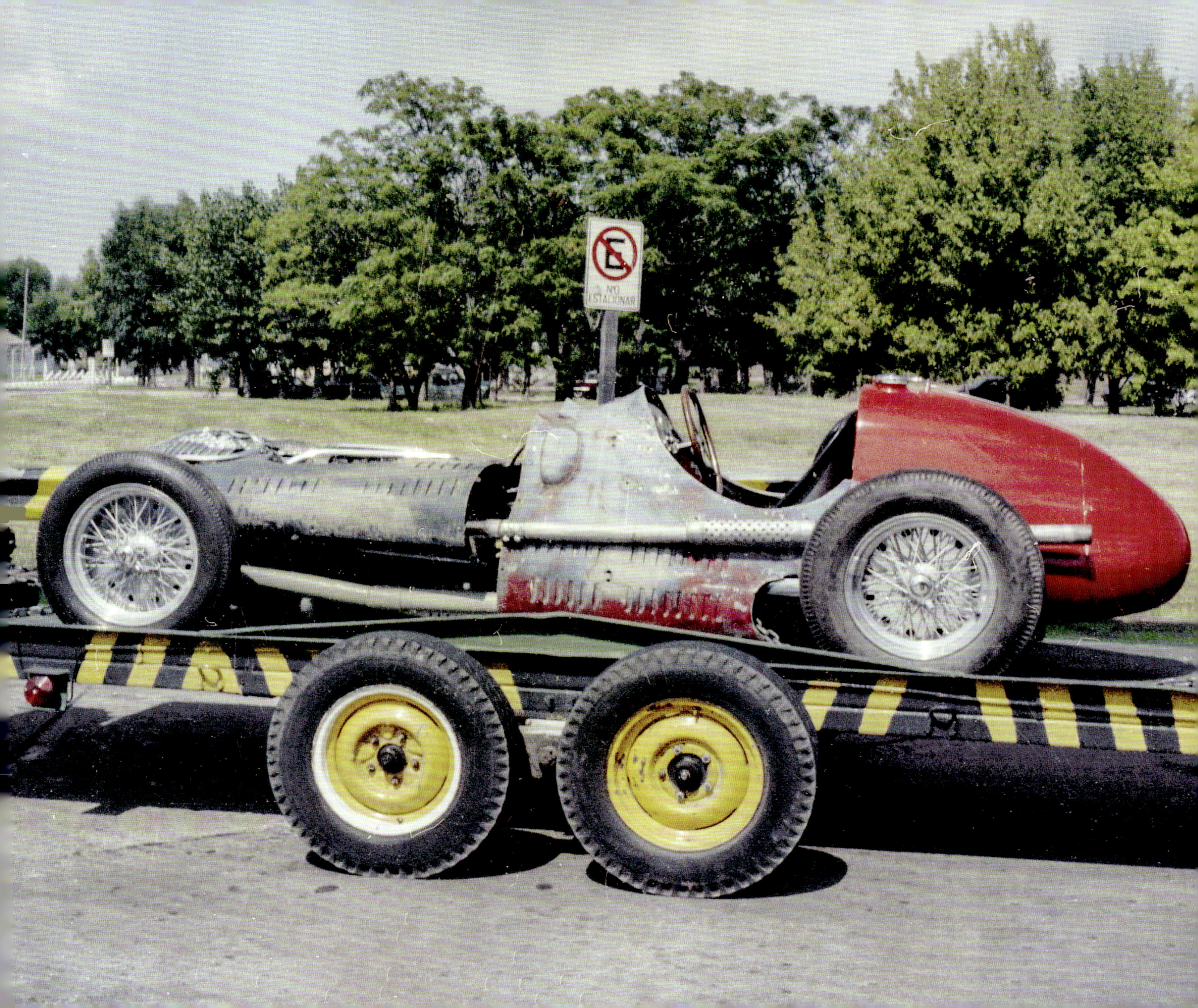
NO ESTACIONAR

Mystery in Argentina

address and identifying the people in the picture: Oscar Martínez, the owner of the shop; with his back to the camera, Antonio Castro known as *El Gallego* who was an amateur racing driver; and of course Bollaert. I found Oscar's phone number and called him. He confirmed that it was him with *El Gallego* and added that he had a workshop just across the street and that Lucio Bollaert used to bring his cars there for repairs and restoration. He did not remember that car specifically but mentioned some that Bollaert had owned, including a Bentley, a Vauxhall and a Grand Prix Bugatti. Suddenly, we were almost in a position to confirm that Bollaert owned a Maserati 4CLT. In those days he had a Peugeot dealership, so the 604 that can be seen in the picture is probably his, and knowing that these cars were imported only for a short period of time, we can conclude that the picture was taken most probably between 1979 and 1982.

Another photograph from the same set shows the car, Lucio Bollaert and Antonio Castro, wearing the same clothes as in the picture in front of Rulemanes Oscar, and another person with the car on a bridge over the Ruta Panamericana km 50, which is near Pilar. Why the car was there is not known.

Then there is the photo of a Maserati on a trailer pulled by an Automóvil Club Argentino truck and looking in poor condition: body panels missing, old and deteriorated paint, and a different radiator. For some time we did not know if it was the same car,

● From the same set of pictures as the one on the previous page, this one confirms the identity of the car, as the plate on the dash clearly reads 1600.
whitefly.cc

Mystery in Argentina

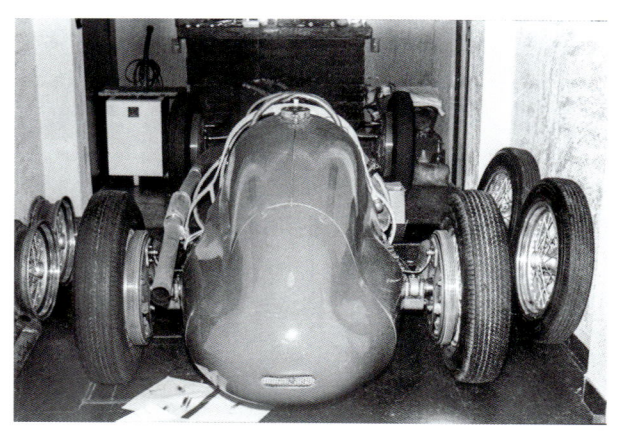

In these pictures the car looks very complete and in one piece, confirming it was restored in Argentina prior to its departure to the US. The location is unknown.
whitefly.cc

Maserati 4CLT

Mystery in Argentina

- Rulemanes Oscar was a shop in Pilar, Buenos Aires, where Lucio Bollaert had a house. Across the street, Antonio Castro had his shop, where Lucio Bollaert used to bring his cars. This picture confirmed that he owned and restored 1600. The man with moustache is Martínez; with blue polo shirt, Bollaert; and leaning into the car, Castro. *whitefly.cc*

mainly because we thought that 1600 had left Argentina without being restored, and compared with the pictures from when Viaggio was racing it is clear that it had been modified. Looking carefully at one of the colour pictures, the chassis number 1600 can be read on the dashboard, so there can be no more doubts about what happened before it was exported. It was owned by Bollaert who brought it to Castro's workshop for restoration and then he sold it. Unfortunately Castro passed away more than a decade ago and Martínez does not remember the car, so the photographic proof is all that we have.

What is probably the last set of pictures of the car in Argentina shows the single-seater in an exhibition at a place called La Rural in the city of Buenos Aires. It looks complete but for the body, and it is clear that a lot of work has been done to bring it back to its original mechanical configuration. It is not known which gearbox and engine was fitted back then, but they look like Maserati items, probably a mix of parts as was very common in the 1970s. The magazine *Trident* in its issue no.23 published a photo with a reference to 1980 which ties perfectly with the conclusions from the other sets of pictures.

Where the engine came from is difficult to know with certainty. When Viaggio bought the car from the Automóvil Club Argentino it was without an engine, because he did not need one. So when Bollaert got the

86 | Exceptional Cars

Mystery in Argentina

car, he might have started the search for an original engine. The dates do not fit very well but there is a possibility that Bollaert had bought one from the ACA during the 1980s. The Ferrari 166FL s/n 011F and its sister car 013F were still with their first owner. The ACA had not only these two cars but lots of Alfa Romeo spares that were sold over the years to drivers and collectors, and some Maserati engines from the 4CLs and 4CLTs. There are some pictures of the Ferrari 011F in one of the warehouses with a twin-stage blown four-cylinder Maserati engine alongside. It is not known if Bollaert obtained one of these but it is certainly possible as the car today has a new engine and another, identified as no.1597, remains with the car, a matching numbers unit for chassis 1600.

I was still trying to understand who bought the car from Bollaert and who its first owner was outside Argentina. In a phone call in July 2018 with Stephen Griswold he confirmed that he had had the car in his California workshop and that it was in such a bad state that the chassis frame was barely in one piece. This might not be accurate as when the car left Argentina it looked half-way restored, so Griswold might have been confused with another one in poor condition. It was many years before.

On the other hand, although 1600's chassis lost its serial number and many other pieces and was modified and fitted with a Ford engine, it kept the original dashboard with the ID plate reading 1600, which is the one fitted to the car today, and was last seen in Argentina in a very correct 4CLT form. So there is no doubt that the people who had the car after Bollaert knew its identity.

On the same day as the previous photo, the car was pictured on one of the bridges of the Ruta Panamericana near Pilar. whitefly.cc

The Maserati at an exhibition in La Rural, Buenos Aires in the 1980s. This is probably the last time it was seen in public in Argentina. Enrique Escobar Tonazzi

Chapter 8
Back to the track

The car surfaced in California with Ben Paul Moser in the early 1980s. By the mid-1980s, it was owned by the noted Japanese collector Yoshiyuki Hayashi who commissioned a complete restoration by Stephen Griswold of Berkeley, California. In a fax dated 29 June 2007, Griswold states, regarding 4CLT1600: 'Ben Moser bought this car from Argentina about 15 years ago and sold it to Hyashi (*sic*). I restored the car for Hayashi'.

In 1995, the car was bought by Bernie Chase from Symbolic Motor Cars in La Jolla who sold it the following year to the United KIngdom. The car was imported on 30 April 1996 by Tony Merrick of Waltham St. Lawrence, England. During September 2018, Adam Ferrington paid a visit to Merrick and they discussed this 4CLT. Tony's notes revealed that he had the car with engine no.1597 for an engine rebuild.

With a freshly-rebuilt engine, the next owner was Peter Rae (a director of Reynard Cars), who kept it unraced until he sold it a few months later, finally to someone who would use it again, French enthusiast Jean-Louis Duret.

Duret acquired 4CLT 1600 in 1996. He entered the car at the first Grand Prix de Monaco Historique in May 1997. The same year he raced in the Oldtimer Grand

● 4CLT 1600 as restored by Stephen Griswold in the 1980s and brought to the UK by Tony Merrick. It was about to re-embark on a racing career in historic events. *Tony Merrick*

● Jean-Louis Duret took 1600 back to the track with spirited performances at Monaco, the Nürburgring and other meetings of the growing historic racing movement. *Ton Blankvoort collection*

88 | Exceptional Cars

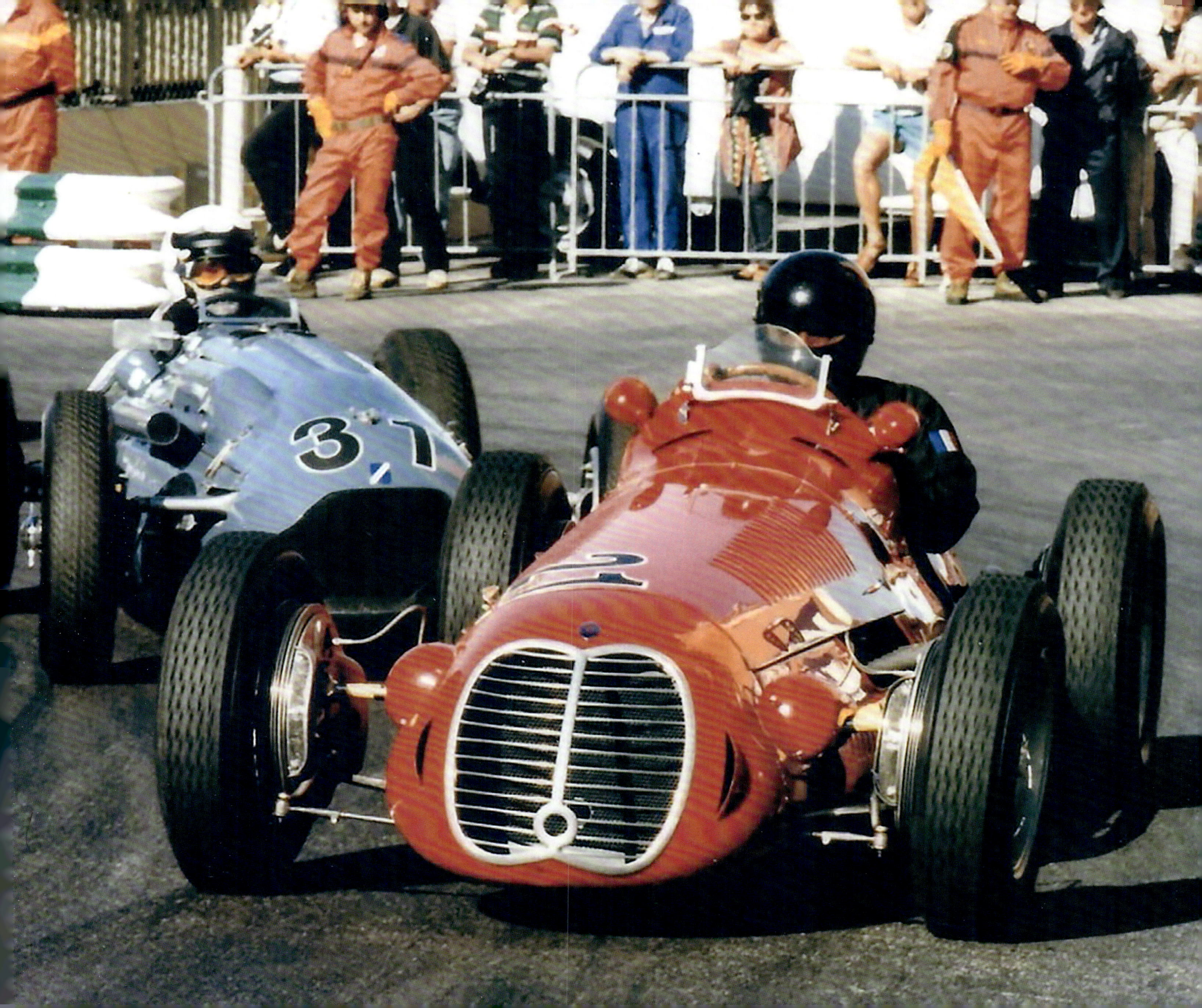
31

Back to the track

● 1600 before it was acquired by Rainer Ott, who undertook further restoration work and the mammoth task of building a completely new engine to the original design.
Tony Merrick

Prix at the Nürburgring and reappeared for the second edition of the Monaco Historique in May 2000. He probably had other racing outings but the last recorded is the Grand Prix de Pau Historique in May 2005. A year later, the car was sold to German Rainer Ott who campaigned it extensively from 2012 to 2015, but the most important thing he did was to re-create the four-cylinder engine and build a batch of five units.

When Ott bought 1600, it was far from being a competitive vintage racer. It needed many hours of set-up work. The motor fitted to the car had the correct matching numbers but it was found to be inappropriate for racing so Ott decided to embark on the ambitious project of building new engines exactly to the original design. The story of this challenge was described by Rainer Ott in a 2014 issue of the Historic Grand Prix Cars Association magazine, and is reproduced here.

Back to the track

San Remo power

Re-creating the Maserati 4 CLT/48 engine
By Rainer Ott

In 2007, I wanted an additional race car, to complement ERA R9B. What fitted the bill better than a Maserati? Finally, I had the choice of two 4CLT/48s. One was race-ready, on the button. The other had a defective engine, and parts of its chassis and body had been modified, but this one interested me more.

The engine was not repairable because its magnesium block was corroded and worn. So I asked some very good people in the UK to build me a complete new one, with superchargers and everything - but nobody wanted to. 'Too difficult, too expensive, a big risk', they said.

Then I asked a friend in Germany who I believed was capable of doing it. He said 'yes' but I said it should not take longer than a year, otherwise I would buy the other car - I wanted to race one before I turned 70! He confirmed, 'yes, one year', so I bought 1600 in September 2007. We quickly discovered that a year to build this complex engine from scratch is impossible. In that time we could perhaps have the casting patterns, if we were lucky. Unfortunately my friend got sick and I had to take sole responsibility...

I realised also that the enormity and cost of the entire project was too great for one person alone, so I looked for partners who also needed engines for their cars, because they would like to keep the originals safe. Finally, I was able to press ahead with building five engines and to amortise not all but an important part of the cost between the investors. At that point everything became too complicated to do it privately, so I established a company, Historace GmbH, to build the engines.

I had just retired after a long working life [Rainer was CEO of a major German aerospace company], so to start a new business was the last thing I intended to do. But it was a must. When developing the engine, each week we hit a new problem. My rationale was, if we could not solve it ourselves, to seek out the best qualified people to help. Here I was looking for small, excellent companies within 30km of home, to enable personal intervention for fast resolution of issues.

Being located in South Germany's Suebian Alb area, close to Stuttgart, there are many small engineering businesses serving Porsche and Mercedes. They were happy to work with 'Maserati' too; however, there was one stumbling block. When they asked me, 'How many thousand units should be manufactured?' I answered, 'Five!' First they thought I meant 5,000, but again I said, 'Only five units from the relevant parts'. And this was the problem.

So I had to convince the managing directors what a wonderful thing it would be to contribute their expertise, so that a unique historic Formula 1 engine could be re-made. I showed them pictures of the car, the engine, Fangio driving this car, etc. Finally, they became very enthusiastic and part of the 'team'. Their input was absolutely vital.

As a starting point I used the original engine from my car. We made drawings and CAD files for CNC machining. Craftsmen created wooden moulds for casting patterns in the traditional way. Gravity sand casting was employed. The original material was no longer available, so we searched for the most appropriate alloys. Making the first cylinder block to meet our quality criteria took six attempts. Casting, machining, cutting up, inspecting, then improving

The 4CLT engine in all its glory – four cylinders, double overhead camshafts, 16 valves, two-stage supercharging and eight-branch exhaust manifold.
Rainier Ott

Maserati 4CLT | 91

Back to the track

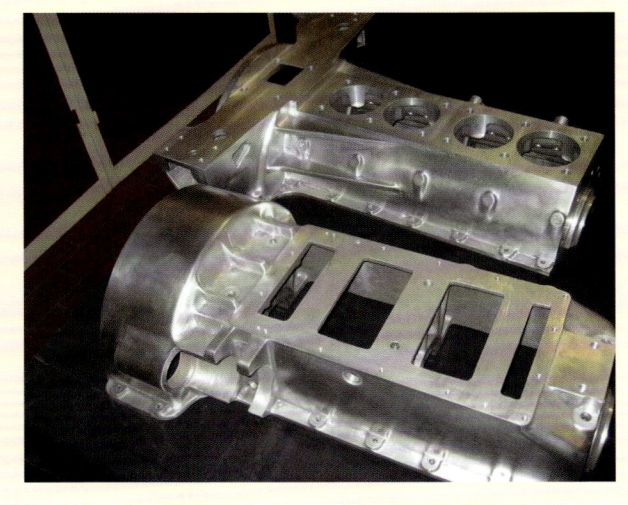

● Building the new engine, clockwise from top left – block castings, the two-cylinder units, crankcase castings, cylinder head showing the four-valves-per-cylinder configuration.
Rainier Ott

and re-mastering the moulds was labour-intensive.

Machined steel and aluminium components were created mostly from our CAD drawings. Machining the cylinder block in one part with the heads was very challenging. Working with our supplier we developed a unique way to machine the combustion chambers, valve seats and channels with a variance of less than 0.01mm between heads. Finally we achieved identical combustion chambers and channels, resulting in smooth and vibration-optimised running.

Casting and machining the water and oil pumps was easier, the challenge here being to define the correct tolerances for impellers and gears. For the crankshaft, con-rods, pistons and camshafts we found suppliers who produced them from our drawings and to our quality requirements.

Making the superchargers, including gears and rotors, was also technically challenging. Here it was very difficult to find first the supplier and then develop the best method of machining, again requiring the highest precision.

Assembling the engine was especially difficult because we had no Maserati know-how. We had to invent things as we progressed, which marque specialists had doubtless already done but not told us. We were delighted that the high level of machining precision enabled our dedicated team to get it oil and water-tight, requiring almost no gaskets.

When, after many setbacks, we entered the phase where the first engine was ready to be run, another series of problems arose. We had the good fortune to be able to use the very modern computer-controlled dynamometer at the Hochschule Ravensburg, the University of Applied Science in the nearby city of Weingarten.

We received enormous assistance from Professor Dr. Michael Pfeiffer and his enthusiastic young engineering students. Within weeks they had studied many books to maximise theoretical knowledge about alcohol-fuelled two-stage supercharged engines.

Their input was fantastic and they were justifiably proud when they saw, and heard, the result of our project together. The university is also successfully developing and building a racecar in the German Formula Student competition.

Naturally, we were nervous in the lead-up to starting our engine for the first time. When I pushed the starter button it turned, but there was no ignition reaction. We reviewed ignition timing, carburettor settings and fuel supply, but again, nothing. Eventually we discovered that the starter motor was turning in the wrong direction. Once corrected, the engine ran, without leaks. We were very happy and thought 'We are almost ready now'.

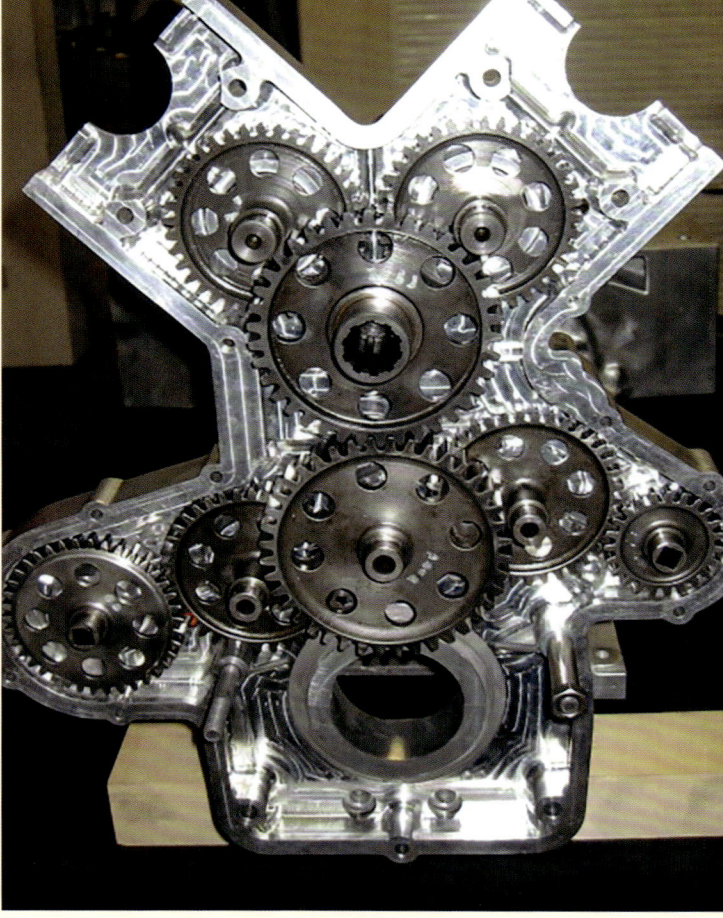

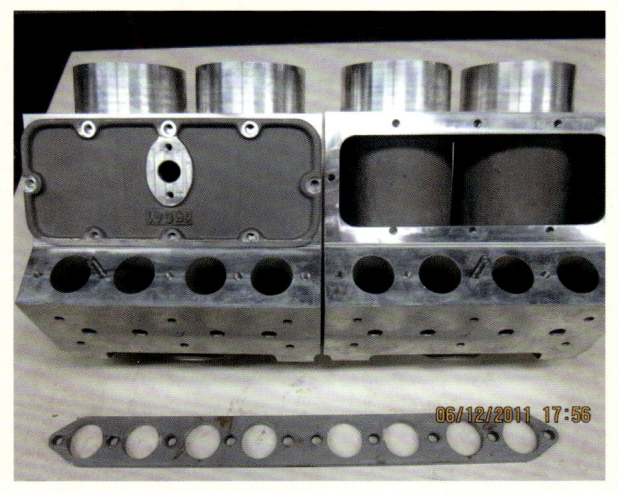

From that long-awaited and very memorable first day, we came up with a slightly disappointing 190bhp and, in the last test run, a holed piston. This was reason enough to work out a Dyno Test Programme, comprising individual test runs for camshaft timing, ignition timing (starting with 28 degrees advance, then 35° and 42°), fuel mixture, carburettor settings (jets from 300 to 550), fuel pressure (0.2 to 0.5 bar), supercharger boost (1.5 to 2.2 bar) and compression ratios (6.0:1 to 7.5:1).

We ran the prototype on the dyno for almost nine months, during which a vast range of ignition and cam timings, compression ratios, supercharger drive ratios, boosts and fuel mixtures were tested using special equipment from the University's engine research department. We were even able to 'look' into the combustion chambers during engine runs. This period of trial and error was at times very frustrating – we strengthened the magneto and had to repair occasional damage - but also exciting. Eventually the results were as well.

Engine internals, newly made with great precision, clockwise from top left – crankshaft and shell bearings, timing gear train, cylinder heads with valves in place, and the two cylinder units pre-assembly. *Rainier Ott*

Maserati 4CLT | 93

Back to the track

The fully assembled engine with the two superchargers in place. In July 2011, Ott's new engine was ready for testing on the dynamometer at Hochschule Ravensburg in Weingarten.
Rainier Ott

None of us would have believed then that it would take another year to come to a more-or-less perfect product, to be installed in the 4CLT for its first outing on a race track, but each parameter had to be tested individually. As progress was slowly made, we measured 210bhp, then 225 and 235, until we recorded our 260bhp target. In later steps we found even more power but we went back to 260bhp at 7,000rpm, to have a reliable engine producing high torque at lower revs.

We also tested different fuel mixtures (85% methanol, 10% benzol, 5% acetone and many ratios in between). We then added water (1%, 3% and 5%) with interesting results, but finally opted for 100% methanol, as we have run in the ERA for a long time.

We found out by accident in one of our last dyno runs that the engine is strong too. I asked the student operator to enter 6,900rpm [maximum]. However, he entered 69,000rpm in error and the computer did what it was asked for. I realised something was wrong when the engine started screaming louder and higher than I had heard before. It sounded like a Stuka aircraft, 300 metres above the ground. When I hit the emergency stop, the log showed almost 10,000rpm - and unbelievable horsepower!

The engine survived, so we know it can stand very high revs. And the higher the revs, the greater the performance. We actually now set the rev limit at a conservative 7,000rpm, at which the engine develops a reliable 260bhp, the figure Maserati always referred to in period, yet we believe was seldom reached.

This prototype has been in my 4CLT from our first outing at the Nürburgring in March 2012 and we made our race début at Dijon in June that summer. It is still running. Only once has it suffered a problem (a cylinder liner slipped, causing some damage, at Pau), but that has been the only failure. It was soon fixed, and the design changed on subsequent engines.

Everything we learned about this engine's development is documented in a thick book. Maybe some people knew this already, but for us it was all new. In another book I have recorded for each individual part all drawings, dimensions, heat treatments, suppliers, order numbers and specialities, in a specific numbered order. Using what I call the Cook Book, the reader could build a 4CLT Maserati engine!

Exceptional Cars

Back to the track

Maserati 4CLT

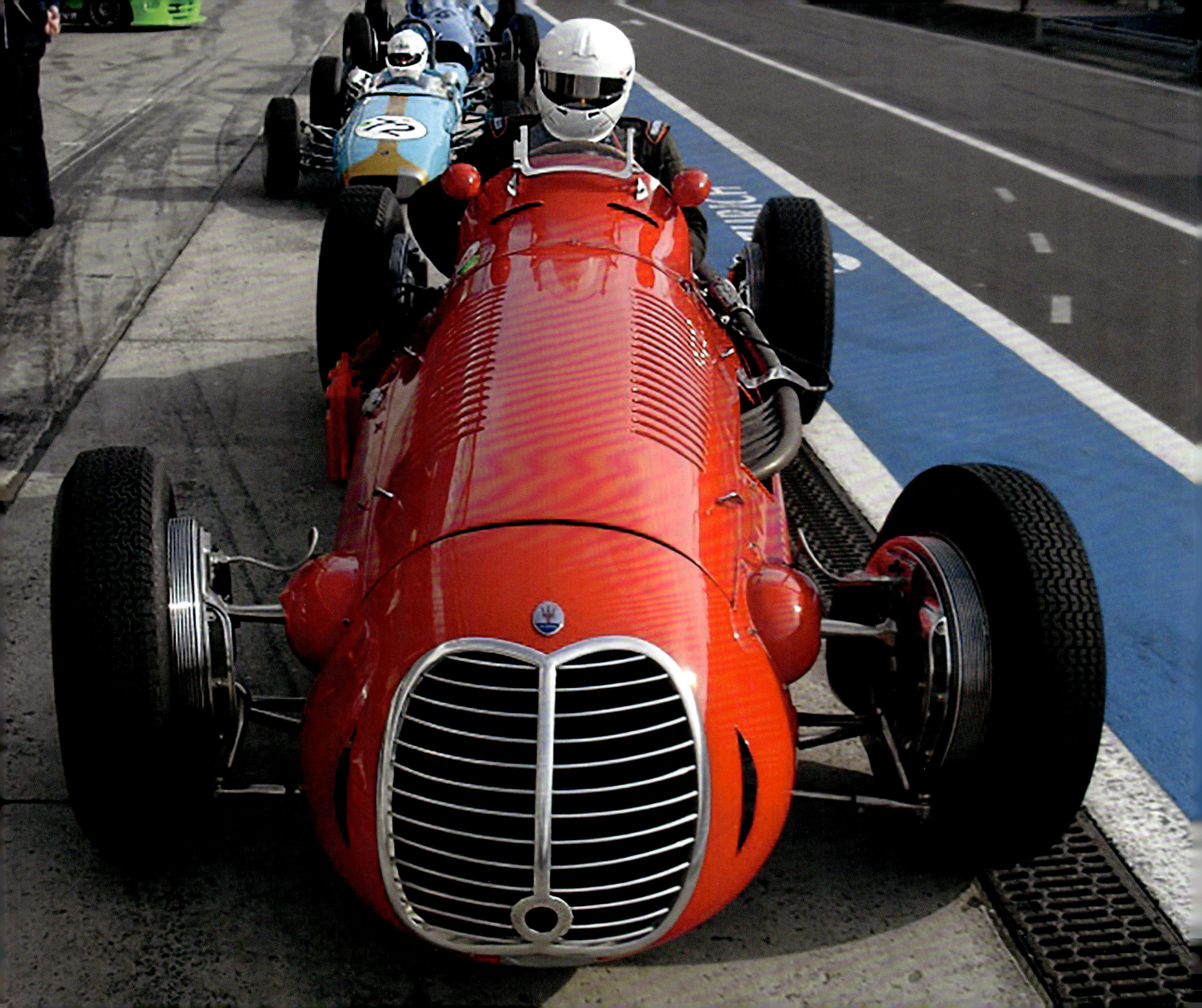

Back to the track

● Moment of truth – Rainer Ott tries the car with its new power unit at a Nürburgring track day in March 2012 (left) and three months later in a race at Dijon (above). The inset picture (right) of original blue paint showing beneath the red is a reminder of 1600's authenticity, 70 years after it was first delivered.
Rainier Ott/Ton Blankvoort

The first public outing for 1600 with its brand new engine was at a track day at the Nürburgring on 17 March 2012. It was an opportunity to test the car and the new power unit and for Ott to start to understand how the 64-year-old car handled. The first race event with the new engine was the Historic Grand Prix at Dijon in June 2012. During that year, Ott drove the Maserati four times, including Nürburgring, the Goodwood Revival, and Imola. Then in 2013 he did five races starting with the Jim Clark Revival in Hockenheim, followed by Pau, the Solitude Revival in Germany, Nürburgring, and Jerez in Spain. For 2014 its programme included the Jim Clark Revival again, Dijon,

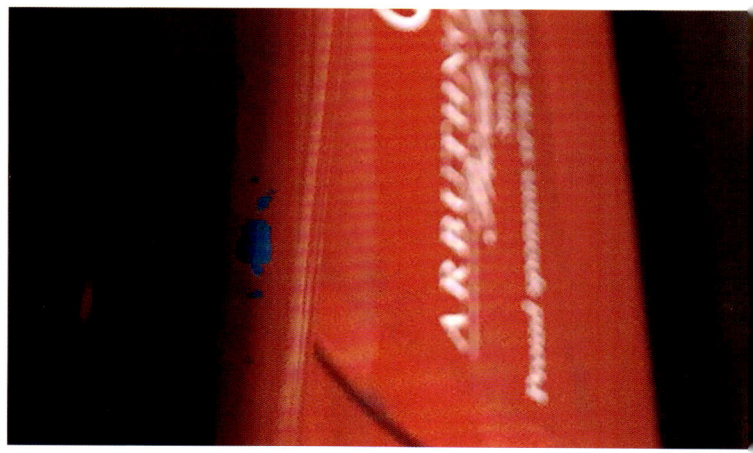

Maserati 4CLT | 97

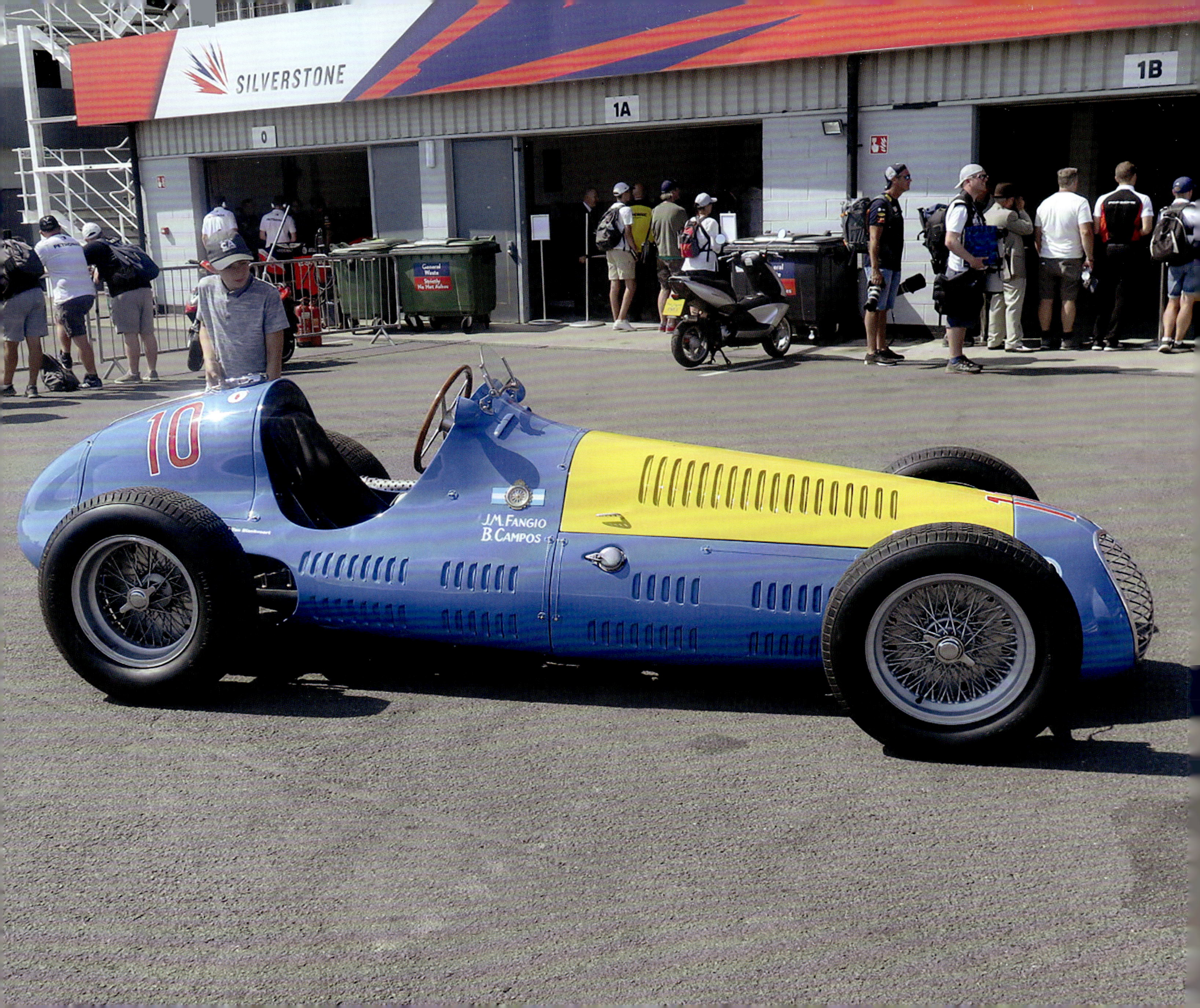
SILVERSTONE
0
1A
1B
10
J.M. Fangio
B. Campos

Back to the track

● Resplendent in Argentine racing colours, 1600 was presented at the 2018 British Grand Prix as part of the celebration of 70 years of racing at Silverstone. Rubén Juan Vázquez and Oscar Espinoza, sons of Juan Manuel Fangio, were invited to autograph the car by its present owner Ton Blankvoort (left) and Rainer Ott (right).
Ray Hutton/Ton Blankvoort collection

the Goodwood Festival of Speed, an appearance at the Formula 1 Grand Prix at Silverstone, the Nürburgring OldTimer Grand Prix and, once again, the Goodwood Revival. The 2015 season was Ott's last with the car and started in Hockenheim, continued at the Nürburgring and finished at the Goodwood Revival.

In 2016 Dutch enthusiast Ton Blankvoort bought the Maserati from Ott and had it painted in the original ACA colours of light blue and yellow. He showed it for the first time at the Formula 1 British Grand Prix in Silverstone in July 2018 and brought together the car and two very special people: Rubén Juan Vázquez and Oscar 'Cacho' Espinoza. These names were unknown to many people but after a long trial which included DNA tests, a judge in Argentina declared them to be sons of the winner of the Grand Prix de Pau in 1950 driving the Maserati 4CLT 1600 - Juan Manuel Fangio.

A couple of weeks later the car re-appeared at the same venue for the Silverstone Classic event, its last public outing for 2018. At the time of writing, it was being prepared for a full season of racing in 2019, wearing the Argentine international colours.

Maserati 4CLT | 99

Chapter 9
Owning and driving 1600
By Rainer Ott

In 2012, four years after I bought it, 4CLT 1600 was ready to drive – but not yet to race. We had a test-run at an old airport near Lake Constance. The car was equipped with a completely new engine, built exactly to the specification of the original.

I still used the old Ferrari gearbox, which had been installed many years ago by one of the previous owners. I ask myself why they did not use the original Maserati gearbox, which was supplied as a spare with the car. It had damaged gears and we repaired it – but it was not ready for this test-run.

The test track on the old airport was 1.5-km long, with a straight of 500m and a few curves. It was full of potholes and overgrown with grass,

Let us first describe the starting procedure. To wake up an engine which uses 100 per cent methanol, with its low calorific value, is not easy, especially in an ambient temperature of 12°C. And because of its two superchargers, there is a long tract from the carburettor to the engine's combustion chambers. So it is important, first to inject normal fuel through the carburettor inlet to get an easily inflammable fuel mixture. This needs the right timing between injection and starting. Over time we developed a certain sequence and we learned how far to push the throttle when cranking. Just pushing the starter knob for the electric starter will not be sufficient to bring the engine to life.

On that first test, finally we managed to get the engine to run – hesitatingly at first, then after a few seconds, loud and clear, spontaneously following throttle commands. Every time we started the engine we were surprised by the extremely loud, screaming noise, running around to find our ear protectors and, through them, experiencing the best engine music you could imagine.

With the engine warmed up, it was time to climb into the car. The cockpit is quite narrow and short. There is not much distance between chest and steering wheel and it is not very comfortable, particularly considering the angle your arms have to adopt. The clutch pedal is on the left side, in the middle between your legs is the gearbox and the brake pedal and the throttle are over on the right

The clutch and brake pedals need a lot of effort to push down, which is difficult because your legs are spread due to the gearbox in the middle, and they are sharply angled because of the short cockpit. The seat is narrow, but holds the body well. Altogether, the seating position is not really convenient – but, hey, it's a race car.

Time to get going. I pressed the clutch and shifted into the first gear, held the engine at 2,000 revs - and it stalled. I learnt that for a race car you need at least 3,500-4,000rpm, then let the clutch pedal go. Then the wheels are spinning; it challenges your skill to minimize the wheelspin for optimum acceleration.

The car jumped away, surprisingly powerful, sliding a little bit sideways. I started to test the brakes, steering and roadholding. I learnt quickly that the brakes and steering were not up to racing requirements. I could not say much about the roadholding as this track was too slow and not appropriate for fast driving sequences but I realized that the front suspension was too soft and there was too much understeer.

Ready to race – Rainer Ott tested 1600 with its new engine on an old airfield before venturing out to public events at Dijon and Goodwood. *Rainier Ott*

100 | Exceptional Cars

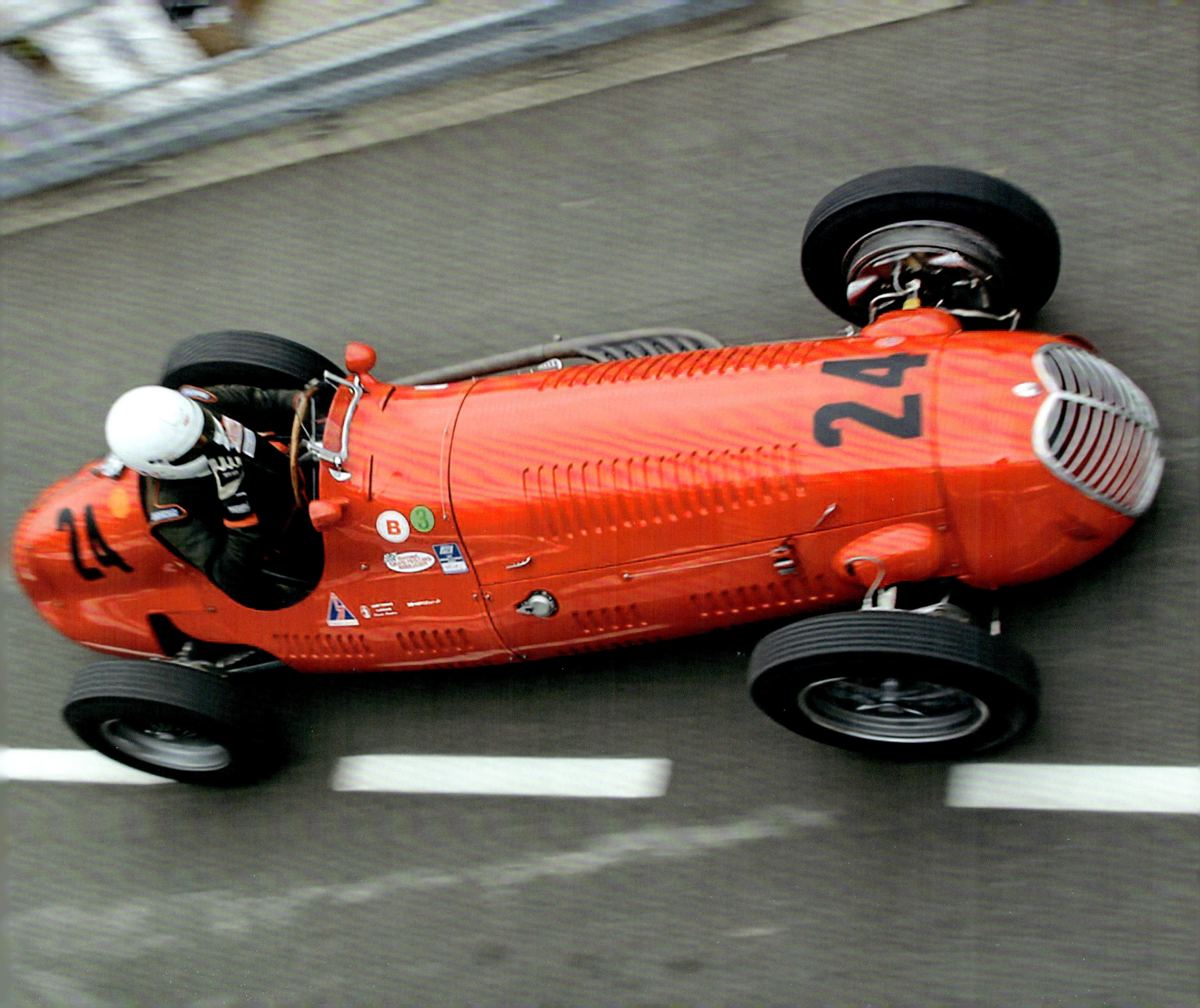
24
24
B
3

Owning and driving 1600

● Race start at the Goodwood Revival meeting 2012. Rainer Ott in 1600, no. 48, got away well but his progress was hampered by the slow and difficult gearbox. *Rainier Ott*

I was not too comfortable driving around this small track, accelerating hard on the short straights, just to slow it down before the next curve with inadequate brakes and then to turn into it using all the power in my arms at the steering wheel. After 25 minutes driving it was clear that there was a lot to do to prepare the car for racing. And I was exhausted.

The Ferrari gearbox was working very well. It was precise, easy, and fast to shift gears. But I planned to install the original Maserati gearbox, which was designed and built by Fiat back in 1928 and used in their cars. Maserati used this slightly modified gearbox for the 4CM, 6CM, 4CL and 4CLT race cars, from 1933 until 1951 – almost 18 years, unbelievable.

The steering system which Maserati used for the 4CLT, is one of the worst they used in their race cars. It is a worm-and-peg system, with nine links and rod-ends between the steering box and front wheels. These links add up to a large amount of play, which does not make for precise steering. This, in combination with the huge effort needed to turn the steering wheel, makes the car almost undriveable. But nevertheless, we have to keep the original steering system, so we manufactured a new and more precise worm-and-peg system and replaced all the rod ends with new, finely-machined competition parts.

The 4CLT braking system was almost unchanged from that of the 4CMs, 6CMs and the 4CLs built between

Owning and driving 1600

1934 and 1939. It has big drums, which is good, but still uses the Simplex system, which does not distribute the full braking power from the linings to the inner brake rings of the drums. This cannot be changed. The only thing to be done is to find the best possible brake linings for it, which is not easy. It requires comprehensive brake testing and adaptation, and precise adjustment of drum and brake lining diameters.

The suspension has to be looked after in detail, especially the shock absorbers. They can be adjusted in three positions and the correct position has to be found by testing the car together with individual springs.

Altogether, it can be said that the design of the 4CLT follows the layout of its pre-war predecessors. With the exception of the chassis and body, it is very similar to the 4CL from 1939, and so it drives correspondingly. Only the stiffer tubular frame chassis, compared with the ladder chassis of the earlier 4CL, enables better roadholding. This new chassis and the more powerful engine with two superchargers makes it considerably faster, but not really better or easier to drive. I think the driver needs to be a bit more courageous than in the 4CL.

After all the improvements and testing, we appeared for our first race with 4CLT 1600 at Dijon in June 2012. As a 4CLT is seldom seen racing, its appearance, and especially the engine noise, was spectacular and there was always a big crowd of people around it in the pits.

During the qualifying I tried to get more used to

Goodwood 2012 - Unfortunately, the gearbox difficulties necessitated a pit stop after six laps.
Rainier Ott

Maserati 4CLT | 103

Owning and driving 1600

● Happy on track – Ott felt that the years of painstaking work on improving the car had paid off. *Rainier Ott*

the car, as far as it was possible in such a short time. Immediately I realized that the Maserati gearbox, now installed, is terrible. The gear lever is between your legs, deep in the cockpit. It is difficult to shift and additionally it requires a lot of effort. The shifting speed is too long and to change down you have to be very precise with the throttle to meet the exact rev level at a specific moment. Double-declutching is not the problem; I am used to it. It is the timing within that to achieve the correct rev limit. This is different from all other cars.

Press the throttle and there is a time lag until the engine responds, because of the long way the fuel mixture has to flow from the carburettor, through the two superchargers and various pipes until it reaches the combustion chamber. This makes it difficult to achieve the correct timing for clutch pedal and throttle.

Then you should not forget to push the brake pedal, because you are near to the next corner and in parallel you have to shift the gear lever to the correct position. It's a bit complicated but a good racer gets used to it…

And then the steering: it is now easier, but still requires a lot of effort although we renewed all the rod-bearings and the links. The problem is caused by the complicated system. Very often you have only one hand for steering and the other to shift gears, which means additional effort. We eventually improved it by shortening the lever directly at the steering box. This helped a lot.

The car was still understeering in long and fast curves, which later would be compensated by further changes to the front coil springs and adjusting the shock absorbers.

Owning and driving 1600

So modifications and more testing were required before we appeared for the next race, the Goodwood Revival meeting. There, for the first time, I had a good feeling for the car. It behaved as it should and was very fast on the Lavant Straight. At the end of this straight they have installed a speed trap and it showed that I reached the highest top speed in qualifying for the Goodwood Trophy. Somebody had a problem with that. So they took me directly from the parc ferme to the scrutineers, who inspected the car, put it on the scales, and found that it was 40kg more than the original spec. They were surprised because they expected the contrary, so they let me go.

The only real problem was the gearbox, which unfortunately cannot be changed. With the Maserati gearbox I lost at least two seconds per lap compared with a Ferrari gearbox. Now I know why the previous owner of the car didn't change it…

The race was at 10am the next morning. Two hours before we started with the final preparation, checking fuel, oil, water, the corresponding pipes and hoses. We finely adjusted the brakes and the shock absorbers and corrected the tyre pressures for the prevailing weather conditions. Thirty minutes before the race, we started the engine, precisely following the procedure we had learned. In spite of the low temperature (12°C), it started immediately. We pushed the car to the assembly area and from there all cars started for the warm-up lap, putting the car in its grid position. Two minutes later the race was on.

I had a fast start, revving the engine to 7,000 and overtaking the cars on the row in front of me in the long first gear. The powerful engine enabled that. But I lost this position as soon as I changed into second gear - it just took too long. So the gearbox issue is a bit frustrating. But I felt great, racing down the straight, sitting in a car which has been driven by Fangio, Campos and González. The narrow seating position, the angled arms and legs, the required effort for steering and braking, nothing bothered me anymore.

As the race went on, I got more used to the car, to its speed and cornering. I was mainly fighting against the ERAs. On the straight I was very fast and competitive, but in the corners I lost too much time.

At the end, the ERAs were the faster cars. I felt I was not at the limit in the corners, and I tried harder. Gear shifting was problematic, as usual; braking was straight and sufficient; steering and turning still improvable. Unfortunately, I had to stop the car after six laps, in eighth position, with gearbox trouble.

Before I raced the 4CLT I competed with an ERA for more than 15 years. In period, the Maseratis were faster. But now we have to see that almost all ERAs were raced year-by-year from the 1930s until today and these cars were continuously developed and improved. This did not happen to the 4CLTs. So today the ERAs are the faster race cars.

Comparing the Maserati 4CLT to the ERA, I can say that the 4CLT reaches a higher top speed and has a better acceleration, but it is much more difficult to

Head down, Ott powers 1600 out of the Goodwood chicane and on to the start-finish straight. On the Lavant Straight it proved to be the fastest car in the Goodwood Trophy race. *Rainier Ott*

Maserati 4CLT | 105

Owning and driving 1600

Owning and driving 1600

Taking the chequered flag after 14 laps at Goodwood. Ott is full of admiration for the men who drove 4CLTs in Grands Prix of three hours or more. Rainier Ott

The competition – 4CLT in company with its arch-rival, the ERA. With experience of both, Ott says that the Maserati is faster but more demanding to drive. Rainier Ott

drive and to get the power down on to the track. The gearbox is the biggest obstacle for better lap times. The steering and turning in is easier and more precise in the ERAs and these days they have better brakes due to the modern improvements. A gearchange in an ERA - with the easy pre-selector gearbox – happens in a fraction of the time of a shift in the 4CLT and this at almost full throttle. In a 4CLT a change from third to second can take three seconds, or even more if you miss the correct rev level. This is the most important disadvantage of the 4CLT and explains why some 6CMs also used pre-selector gearboxes for a while, although they were not original.

There is no question that the roadholding of the 4CLT, with its rigid tubular frame, is far better. It has the driving characteristics of a modern chassis. However, if you exceed the limit of grip only a little you will lose the car and spin; only race experience can tell you where those limits are. The ERA with its old-fashioned ladder chassis, is much more controllable. It gives you notice that you are in trouble and you can do something about it; for example, give some throttle to stabilize the rear axle. This compensates for its roadholding disadvantage to some extent.

In the same year I had the chance to drive a Maserati 250F at the Nürburgring. It is a completely different car from the 4CLT. You realize that the 250F has a modern design. You feel it at speed, turning-in and braking. It is not really more powerful, but there are none of the problems concerning steering, braking and gear shifting, so it is much faster. The cockpit is larger and the steering wheel and pedals are better positioned.

In a 250F, you are more a racer, while in a 4CLT you are more a bold fighter. However, I can sum up the Maserati 4CLT thus: it is great to race such a spectacular car. Sitting in it, you smell race history. But racing a 4CLT is a very demanding job. It needs a very experienced, skilled and courageous race driver to race this car seriously and drive it at its limit. We have to admire men like Fangio, Campos and González who drove these cars in races of several hundred kilometres and won.

Chapter 10
Photo gallery

These fine studio images were produced by the Dutch photographer Pim van der Maden and show 4CLT 1600 as presented in 2018 by owner Ton Blankvoort.

The car's specification has been returned as far as possible to that of the 1950 season when it achieved its greatest success. The blue and yellow colour scheme is correct for the national racing colours of Argentina and the names Fangio and Campos have been added as a tribute to its main drivers in two seasons of racing in Europe.

Looking through the pictures in earlier chapters of the car in its heyday, it is clear that it was never as immaculate as it is today. In the immediate post-war years, racing cars were simply tools to do a job – win races – and wore their scuffs and scars from race to race. When they were no longer up to the job they were discarded, sometimes modified for another purpose, or left to rot. Only in more recent times has the historic car movement sought to revive, restore and celebrate them as objects of mechanical beauty. As these photos show, Maserati 4CLT 1600 is a prime example.

- The dashboard identification plate that stayed with 1600 through its years of racing, storage, restoration and revival.

Enthusiasts regard the Maserati 4CLT as the archetypical single-seater racing car of the 1940s and early 1950s.

108 | Exceptional Cars

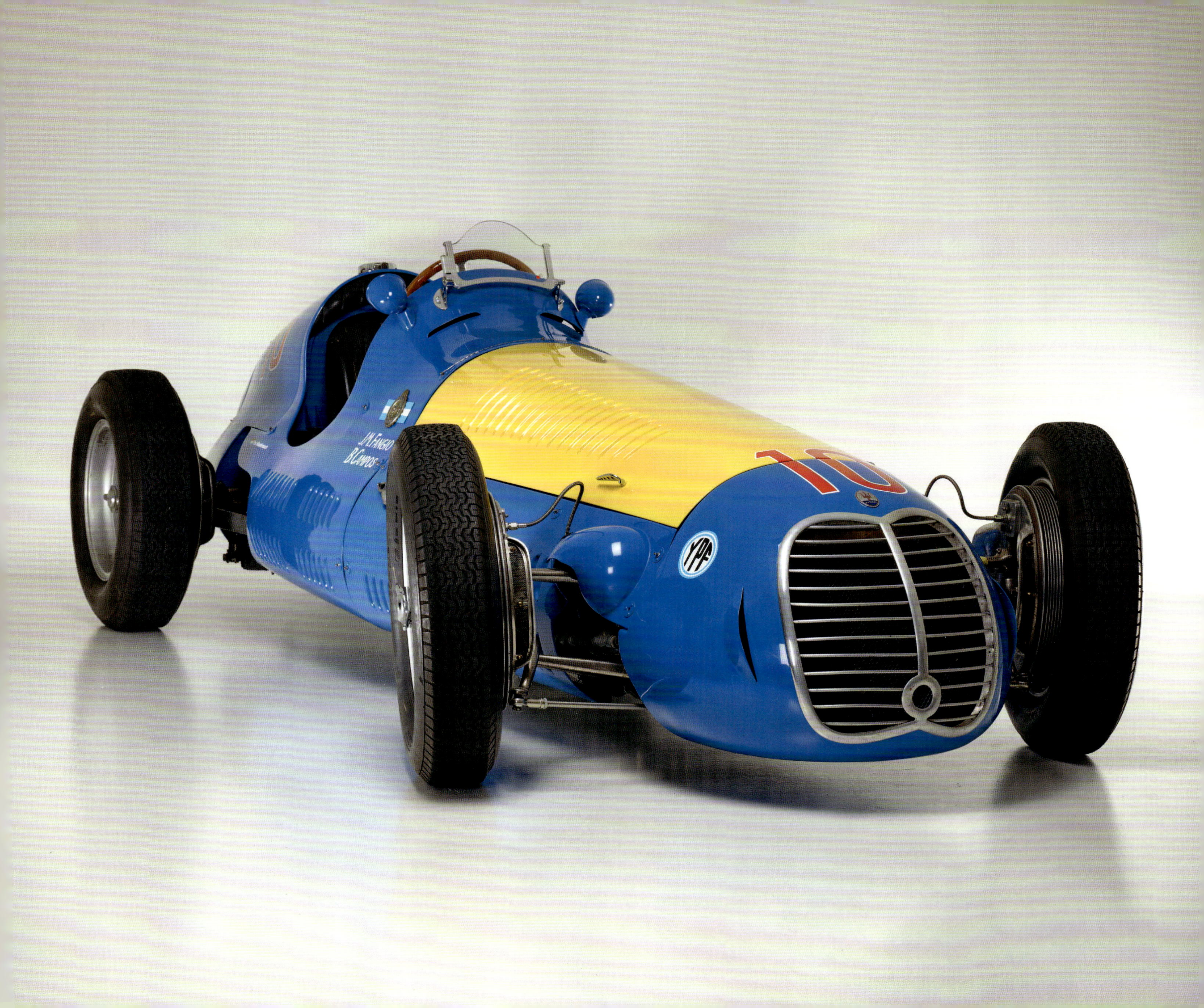
J.M. FANGIO
B.CAMPOS
10
YPF

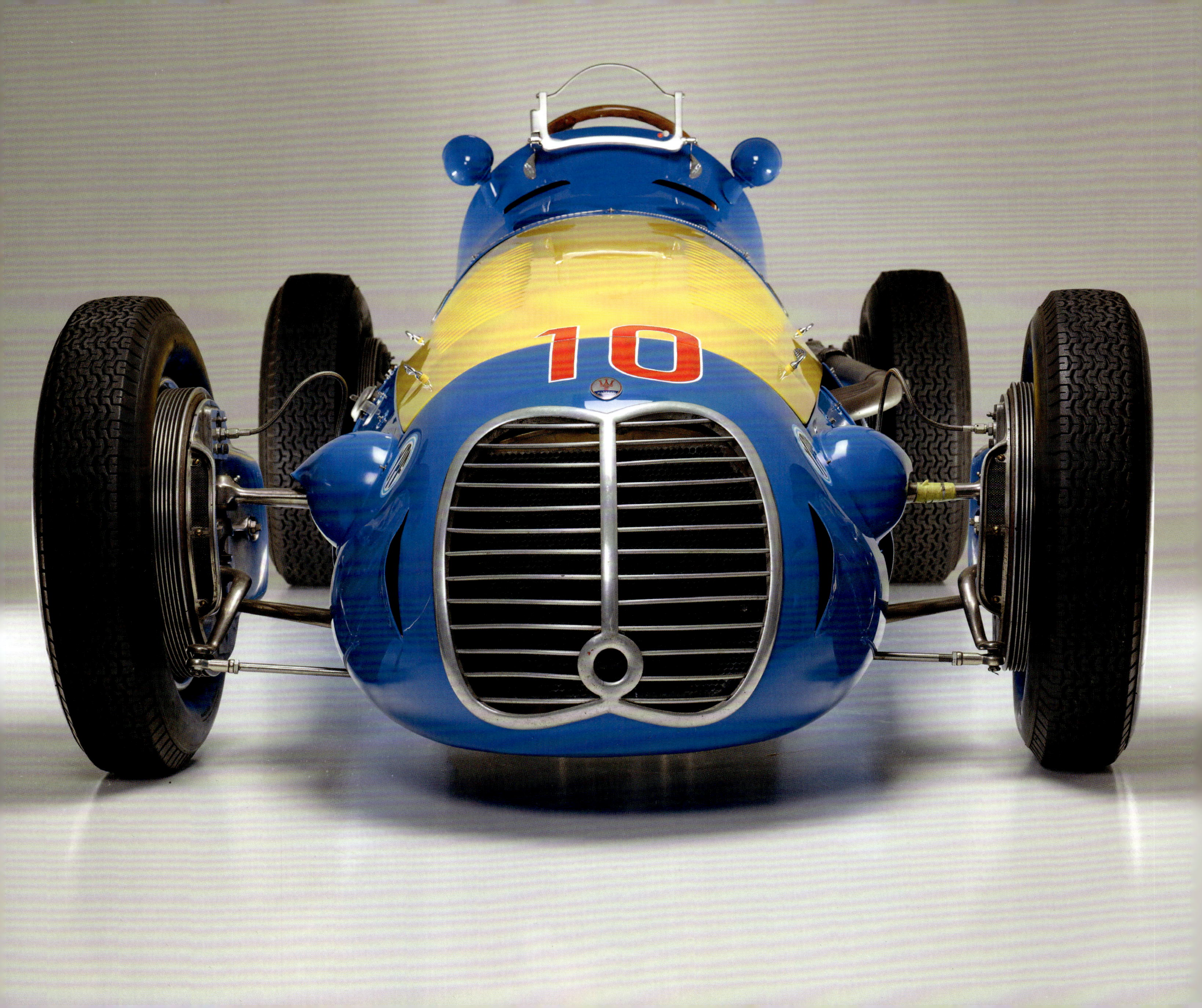
10

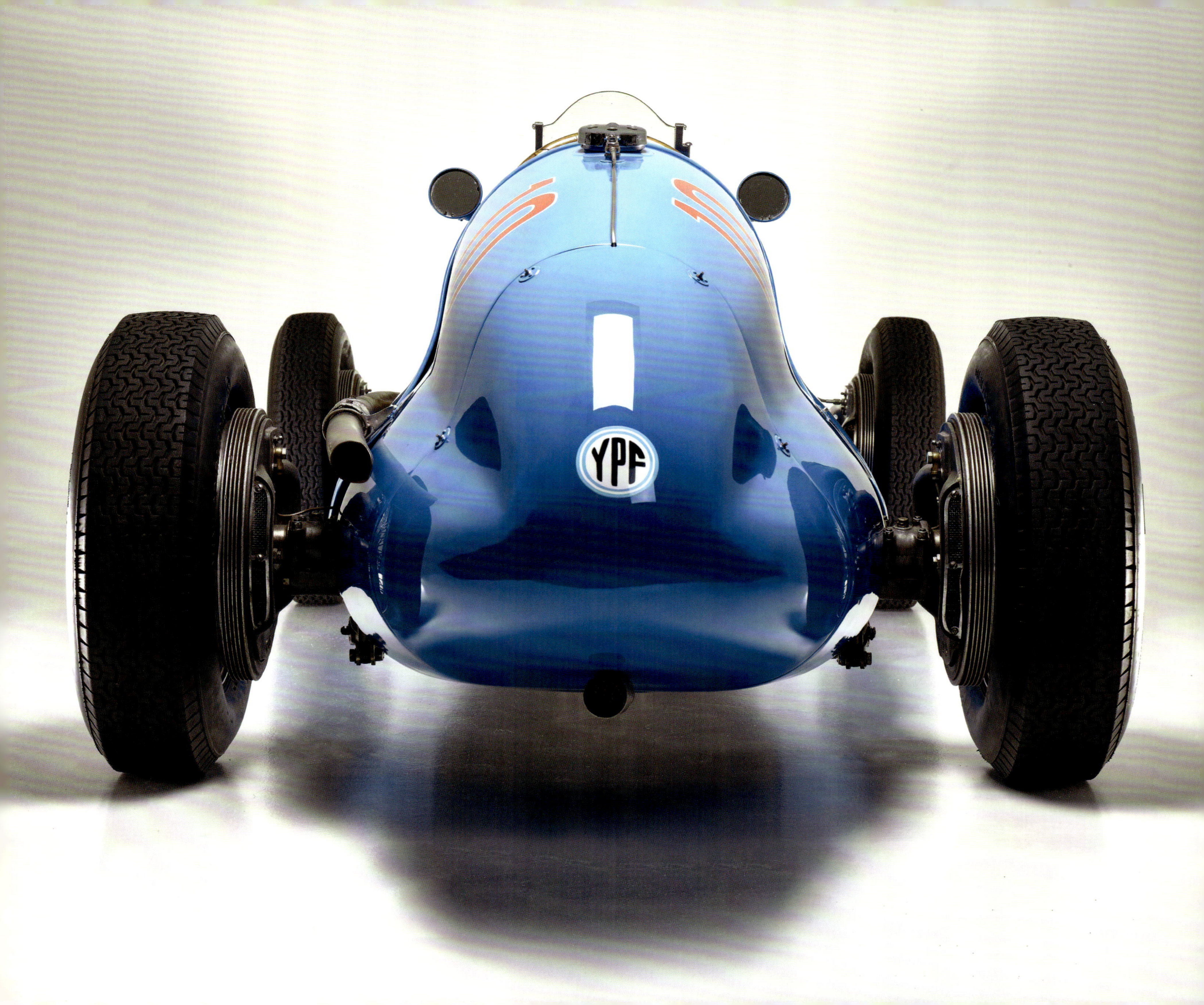
YPF

● The engine may have only four cylinders but it is an impressive sight, with its twin overhead camshafts, eight exhaust manifolds and all the pipework for the twin superchargers.

The stamped number 1597 confirms the original engine supplied with 1600. The current owner also has one of the newly-built 4CLT engines produced by Rainer Ott (see page 91).

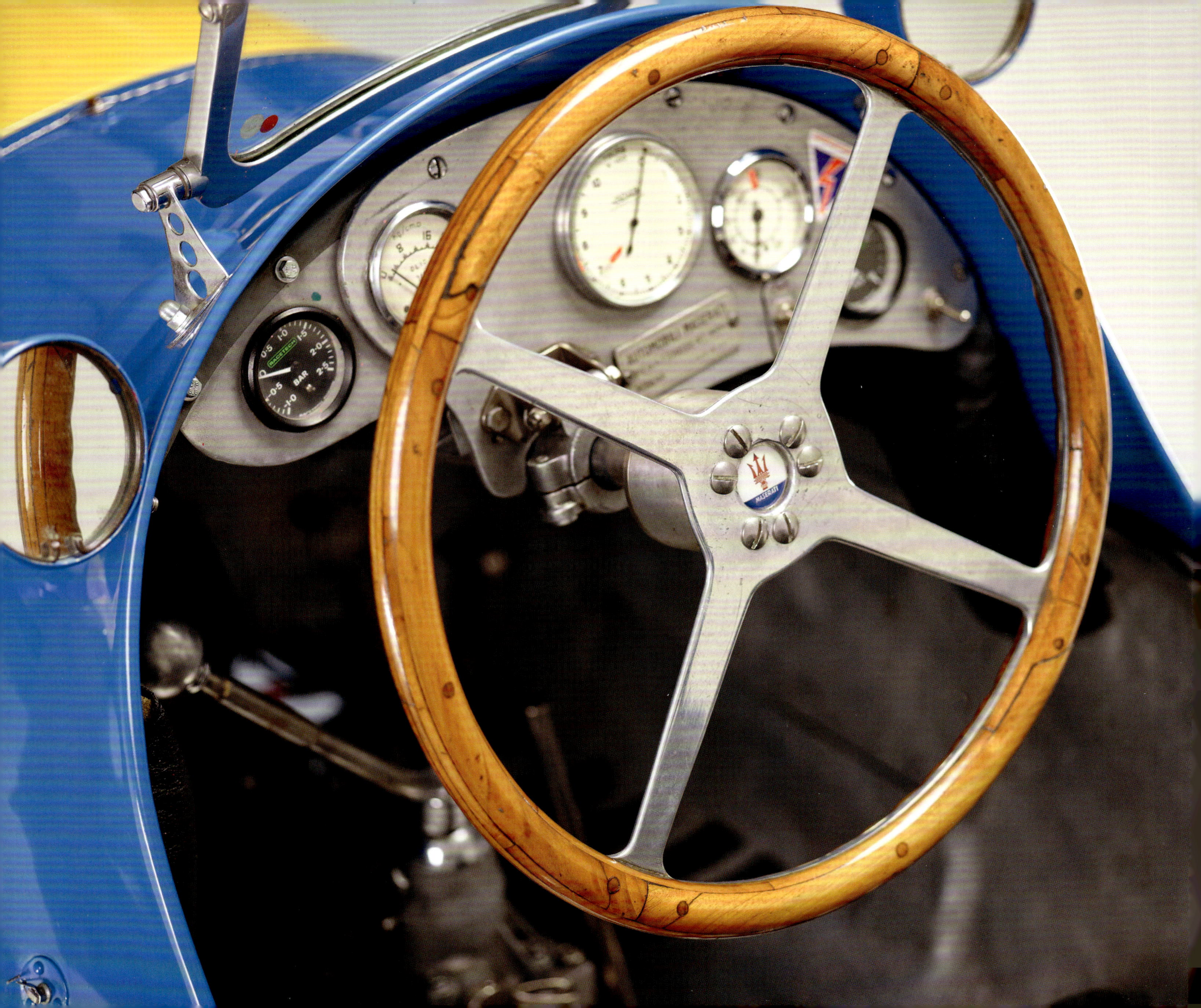
BAR

- Cockpit with its characteristic half-arc instrument panel and four-spoke wood-rimmed steering wheel is a tight fit. Pedals, above, are arranged either side of the gearbox; brake and accelerator on the right.

The gear-lever sprouts from the top of the gearbox between the driver's legs and is operated from the left-hand side. Cream-faced instruments are original; black-rimmed supplementaries are a modern addition to monitor engine performance.

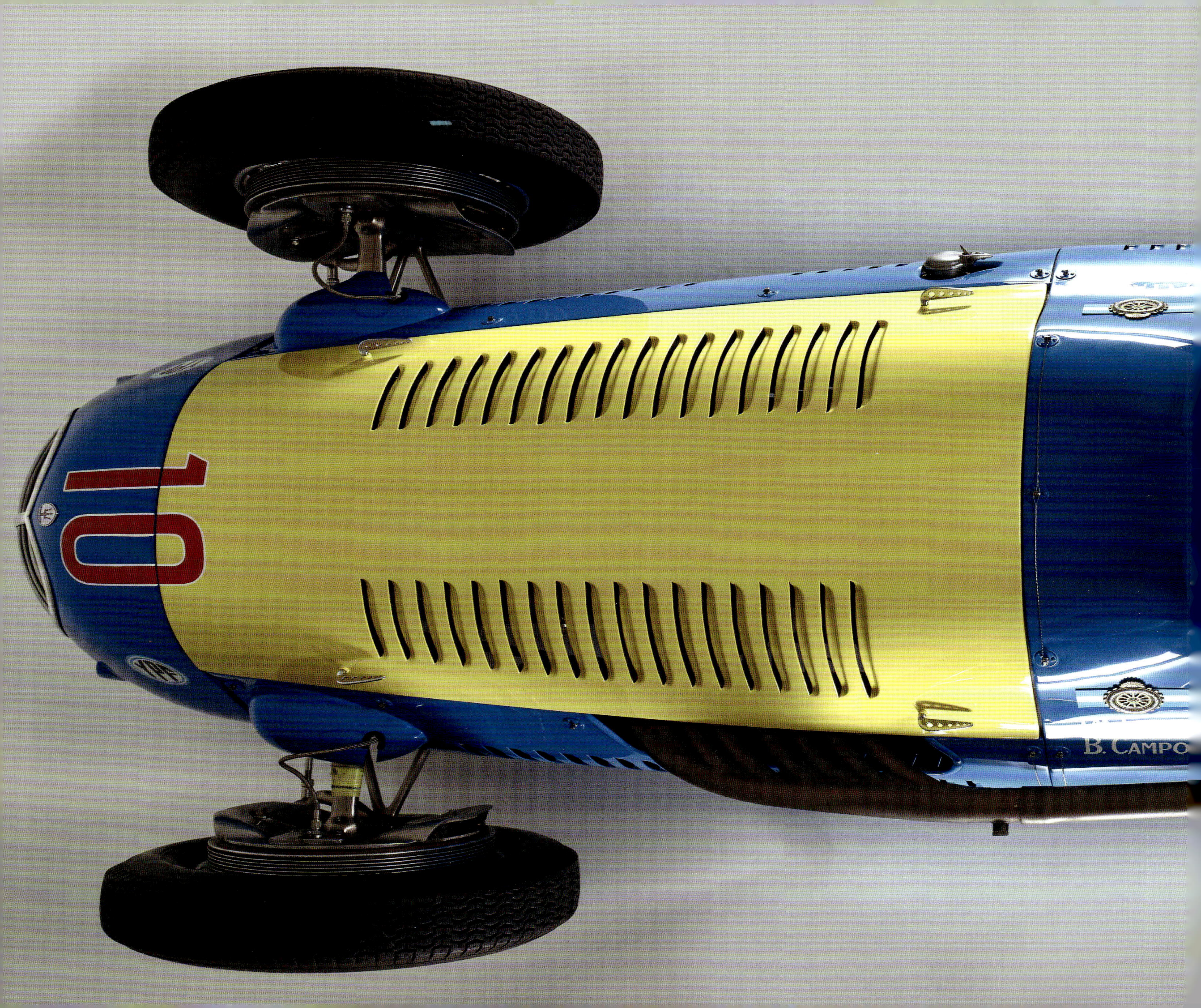
10
B. Campo

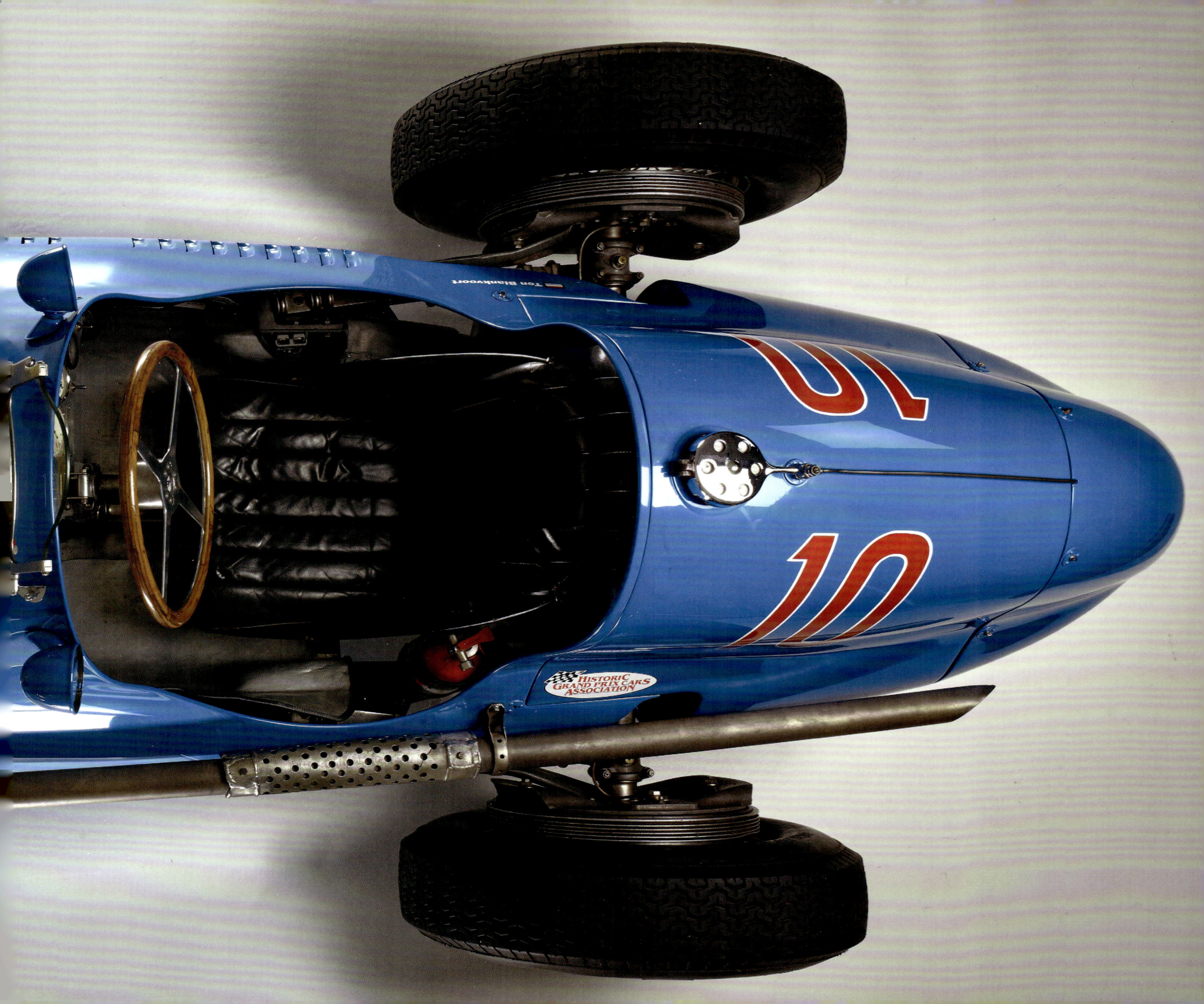
Ton Blankvoort
10
10
HISTORIC GRAND PRIX CARS ASSOCIATION

● Attention to detail – wire-secured fasteners are period, as is the ACA symbol. The elaborate exhaust system fooled many onlookers into thinking that the car has an eight-cylinder engine!

Tight space in the cockpit ●
makes the perforated
exhaust guard, right,
essential to avoid burnt
elbows. Finned brake drums
inboard from the wheels
are a fairly effective way of
cooling the brakes.

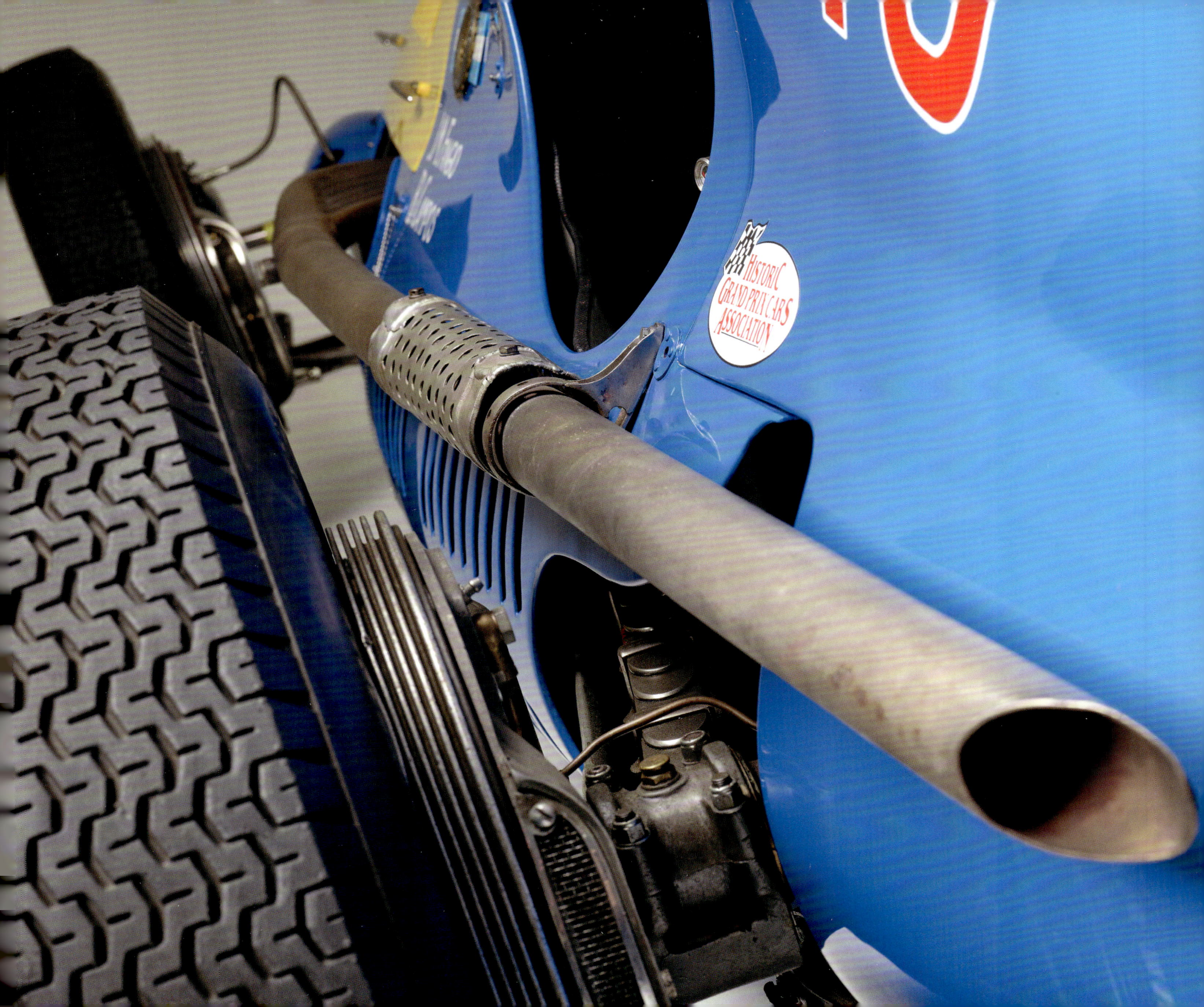
HISTORIC
GRAND PRIX CARS
ASSOCIATION

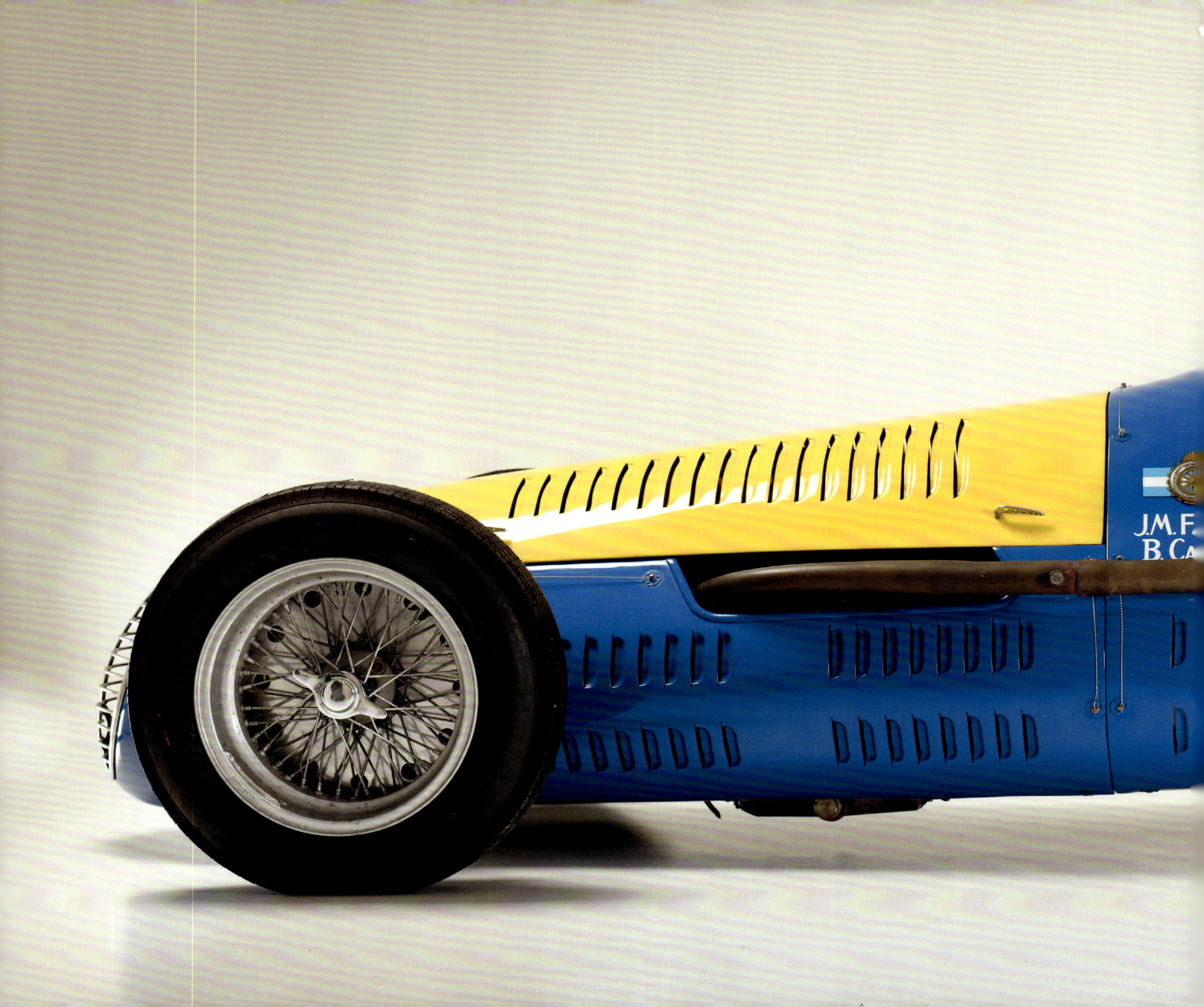

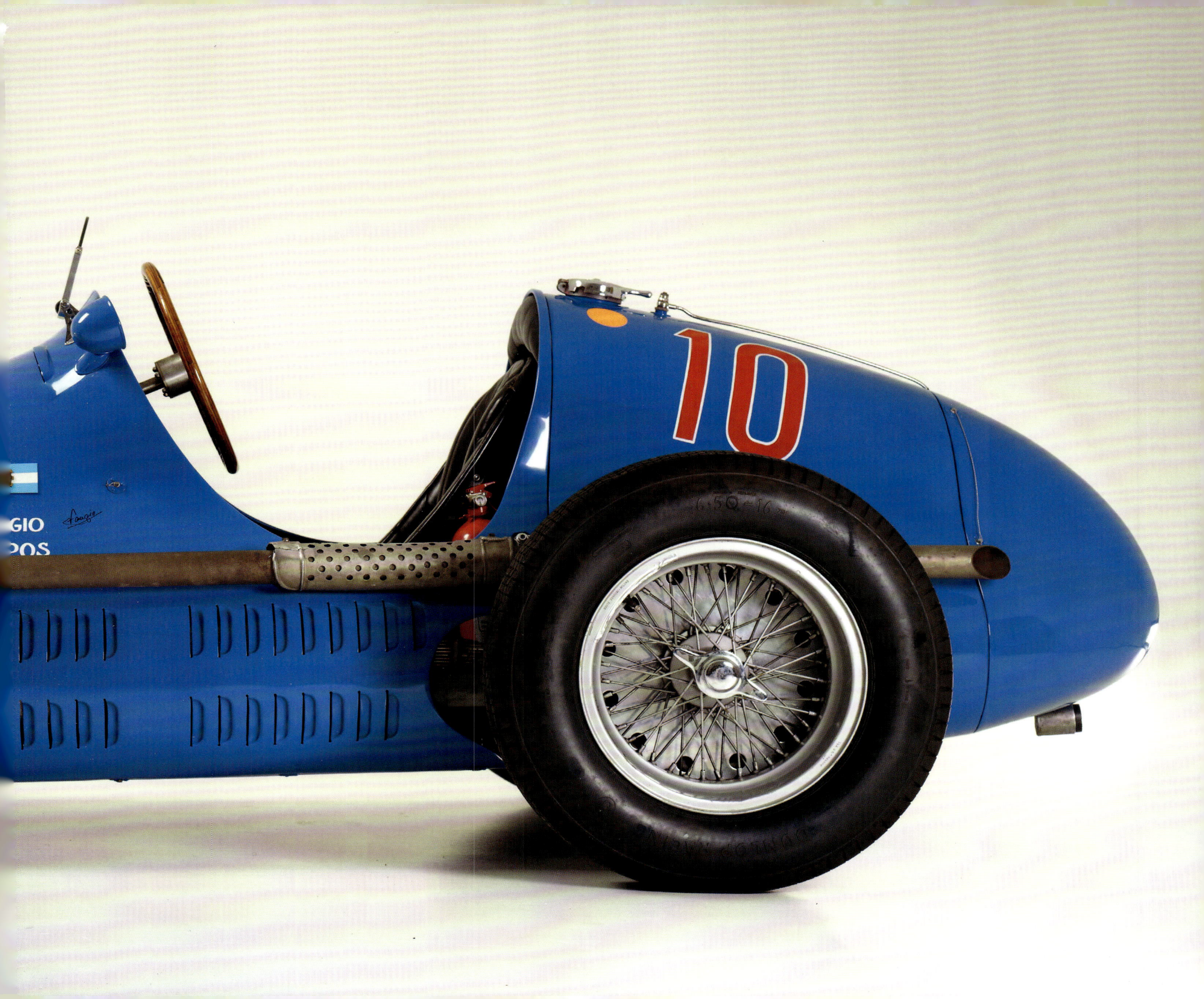
10

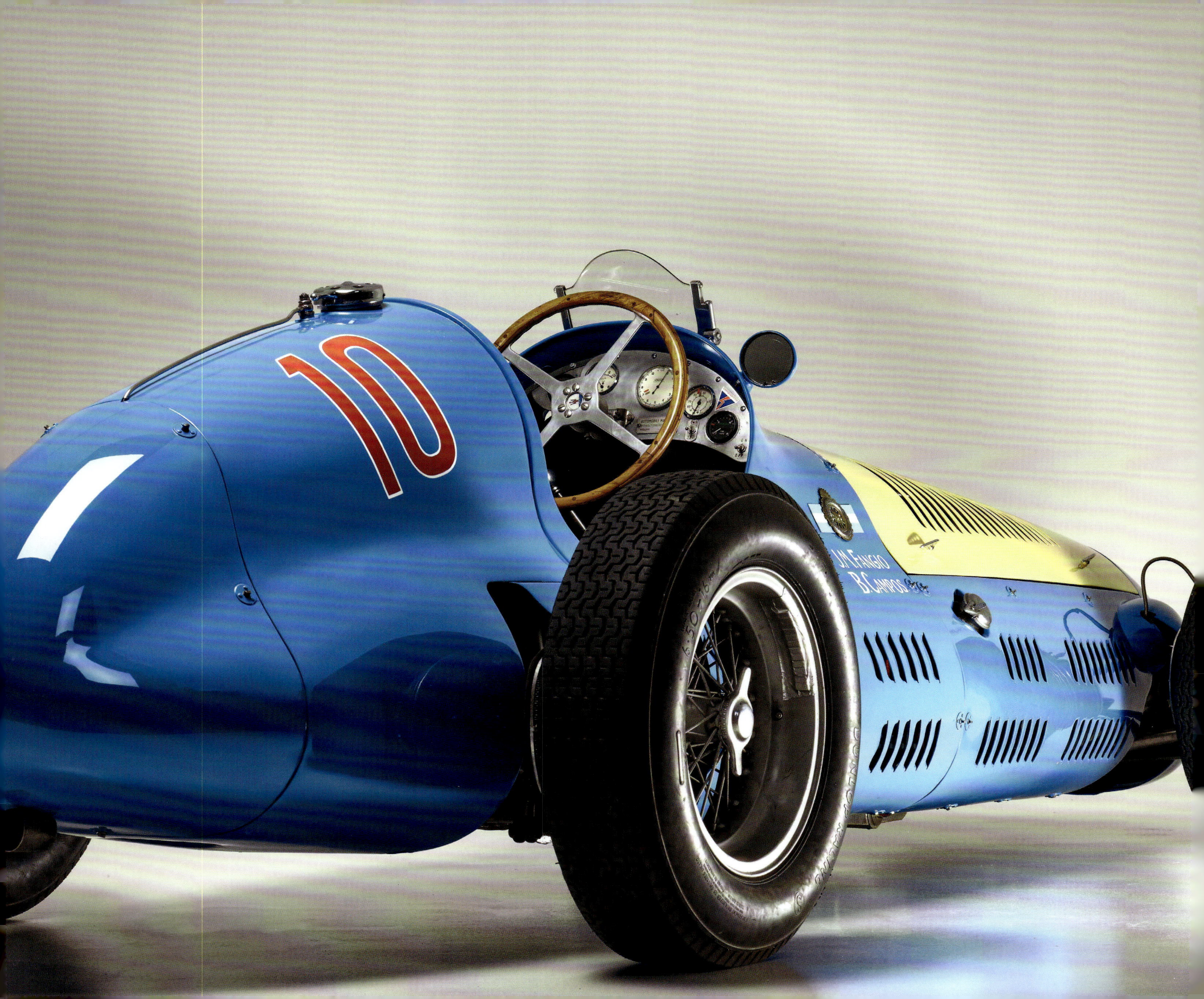
10
J.M. Fangio
B. Campos

● Fuel filler is above the tail tank, immediately behind the driver's seat. The oil tank filler was relocated on the body side, just ahead of the cockpit, as part of the 1950 modifications.

Bucket seat provides good location for the driver and is supplemented by leather-covered padding in the top of the tail section. ●

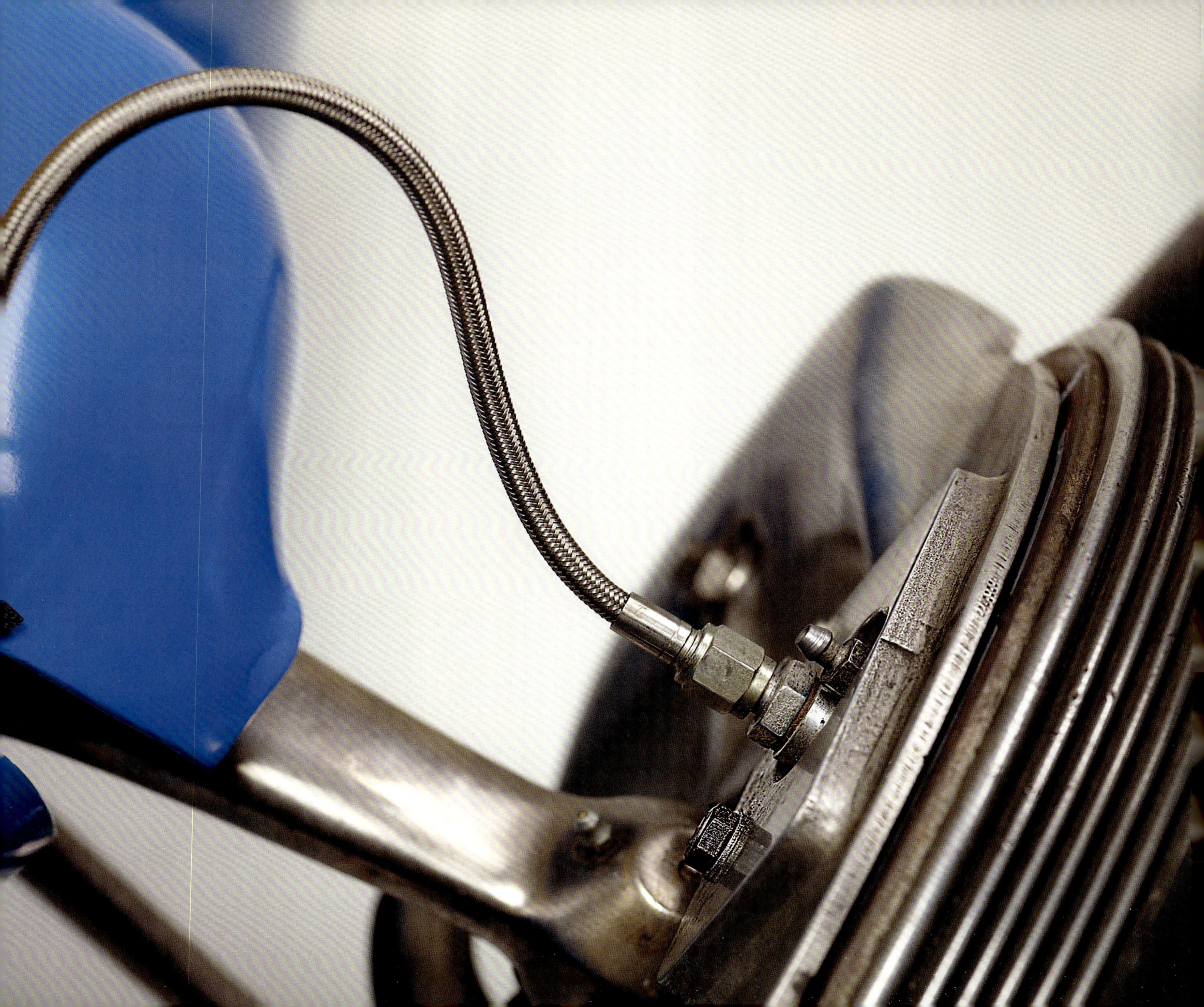

● Armoured hydraulic piping to the front brakes, left, and substantial front wishbones; the coil springs are inboard, operated by rockers.

Rear suspension, above ● and right, is by angled leaf springs mounted direct to the axle. Wire-spoked wheels with knock-on hubs were standard fit for race cars of this era.

Acknowledgements

Club Alfa Romeo Argentina
Gabriel De Meurville
El judío y el goi
Manuel Eliçabe
Ricardo Estévez
Adam Ferrington
Alejandro García del Bo
Gasoleros Group
Coto Girelli
Estanislao María Iacona
Guillermo Segundo Iacona
Valeria Lamas
Roberto Landler
Oscar Martínez
Simon Moore
Rainer Ott
Mauricio Parra
Carlos Quintana
Claudio Scalise
Michael Turner
Alejandro Varalla
Coca Viaggio
Evelyn von Brocke
Ted Walker
Carlos Walmsley
Fredy Yantorno

Archives
Automóvil Club Argentino
Autotest
Carlos Quintana
Enrique Escobar Tonazzi
Gamma-Keystone Collection / Getty Images
GP Library
Héctor Díaz
The Klemantaski Collection
LAT Images
Lorenzo Echeverría
Museo Juan Manuel Fangio
Pim van der Maden
Popperfoto / Getty Images
Rugir de Motores
Spitzley Zagari Archive
Tony Merrick
Vicente Álvarez
whitefly.cc

Magazines
Coche a la Vista
Corsa
Parabrisas Corsa
Rugir de Motores
Trident
Velocidad